W9-CNG-587

AN INTRODUCTION TO PHILOSOPHY

AN INTRODUCTION TO PHILOSOPHY

BY

JACQUES MARITAIN

TRANSLATED BY

E. I. WATKIN

NEW YORK

SHEED & WARD

Made and Printed in Great Britain by
Hazell, Watson & Viney, Ltd., London and Aylesbury

PUBLISHER'S NOTE

THE French edition of this work, under the title Introduction Générale à la Philosophie, *appears as the first volume of seven, which deal with Formal Logic, Theories of Knowledge, Cosmology, Psychology, Metaphysics, Ethics, Æsthetics, and the History of Philosophy. But, since six out of the seven volumes remain to be written, it has been thought better to issue the present volume quite independently.*

The series as a whole is intended to provide text-books for a regular university course as it is found in France, and with that particular end in view prints in larger type those paragraphs which the student should read first, and in smaller type those paragraphs which are merely explanatory or expansive of them. This schematising has been abandoned to make the volume serve for general readers, no university course being envisaged in England or America.

The translation has been made from the eleventh French edition.

PREFACE

My chief aim in composing an *Elements of Philosophy* series, to which this book may serve as an introduction, is to give a faithful presentation of the system of Aristotle and St. Thomas, and in its light to judge the important systems which have followed each other during the last three centuries and the principal problems discussed by modern philosophy. I have tried to adapt the method of exposition to contemporary conditions, and in particular have followed of set purpose a progressive order of exposition—as far as possible the order of intellectual discovery—never appealing to any truth not already known and understood, and never introducing a new notion or proposition for which the way has not been prepared by those which have gone before it and led up to it. The method has obliged me to depart on several points from the procedure of the traditional text-books—above all, considerably to magnify the importance and extend the scope of this Introduction. Yet, thus, I have but returned to the method followed by Aristotle himself. The first three books of his *Metaphysics* are, in fact, nothing but an extensive introduction.

A work of this kind, if it is to be thorough, demands the detailed discussion of certain points, without which the study it seeks to promote would lose all its value as a mental discipline. I should be untrue to traditional philosophy if I reduced it to a few main theses which have lost their freshness, and a few commonplaces of a spiritualist metaphysic, and neglected to bring out its fine intellectual contours and display its power of penetrating analysis.

The present work is intended for beginners. It can therefore make no attempt to reproduce the depth or the wealth of subtle dialectic to be found in treatises written for specialists, and remains strictly elementary. It must, however, preserve the scientific character proper to a philosophical exposition.

Some readers may take alarm at scholastic terminology. Yet no science, no discipline, no form of sport, even, or industry, can dispense with a special terminology—often far more arid and artificial than the vocabulary of philosophy. To require that philosophers should use everyday language implies that their science is just an enterprising topic of conversation, idle arm-chair speculation for after dinner. On the other hand, it may legitimately be demanded that no technical term be used until it has been clearly defined.

. . . . .

Finally, I would say that, if the philosophy of Aristotle, as revived and enriched by St. Thomas and his school, may rightly be called *the Christian philosophy*, both because the Church is never weary of putting it forward as the only true philosophy and because it harmonises perfectly with the truths of faith, nevertheless it is not proposed here for the reader's acceptance because it is Christian, but because it is demonstrably true. This agreement between a philosophic system founded by a pagan and the dogmas of revelation is no doubt an external sign, an extra-philosophic guarantee of its truth ; but it is not from its agreement with the Faith, but from its own rational evidence, that it derives its authority as a philosophy.

Nevertheless, reason and faith, while distinct, are not separate, and, since I am writing principally for Christian readers, I have not denied myself an occasional reference to knowledge familiar to every Catholic, or to certain theological applications of philosophic principles, the better to put philosophy in its proper place in Christian minds, or to help them to maintain the unity of their thought. The fact remains that in our arguments and in the very structure of our exposition of philosophy, it is not faith, but reason, and reason alone, which occupies the entire ground and holds undivided sway.

CONTENTS

CONTENTS

CONTENTS

PART TWO

THE CLASSIFICATION OF PHILOSOPHY

13

CONTENTS

CONTENTS

CONTENTS

INTRODUCTORY

PHILOSOPHERS were once called wise men. It was Pythagoras who first invented the term *philosophy* (φιλία τῆς σοφιάς, love of wisdom),[1] observing that wisdom belongs in the strict sense to God alone, and for that reason not wishing to be called a wise man, but simply a friend or lover of wisdom. His modesty was itself a mark of great wisdom, for the sublimity and difficulty of the highest truths, and the weakness of our nature " in so many respects enslaved," forbid man to acquire " a property right in wisdom "[2] such that he can employ it in entire freedom. As a result of the many necessities to which he is subject, he holds it only by an insecure title, so that he may be termed not wise, but far more truly a beggar at wisdom's door. Nevertheless philosophy is nothing other than wisdom itself so far as it is accessible to human nature.

It is not a wisdom supernaturally infused into our souls which man possesses in virtue of a superhuman illumination. Neither is it a wisdom wholly spontaneous and unconscious (such as within its limits is the prudence of animals, and even the wisdom of simple souls), which he possesses in virtue of a natural instinct. It is the wisdom of man as man, which he

[1] Cicero, *Tusc.*, v. 8 ; *cf.* Diogenes Laertius, i, 12.
[2] Aristotle, *Metaph.* i, 2, 982 b. St. Thomas, *In I Metaph.*, l. 3. *Cf. De Veritate*, q., 7, a. 7.

acquires by the labour of his intellect, and it is for that very reason that his wisdom is gained with such difficulty and held so insecurely, and that those who seek it should be called philosophers rather than wise men.

Such is the nature of philosophy derived from the etymology of the term and its employment in ordinary speech. A philosopher is a man humanly wise. And the man who devotes himself to philosophy, by so doing undertakes to show his fellows the sublimest views at which man's understanding can arrive of the great problems which solicit the mind of the race.

The definition of philosophy as " human wisdom " is still a superficial definition, and a nominal definition, which simply renders agreement possible as to the sense of the term. To attain a more profound definition, a real definition which reveals the nature of the object, we shall study in the sequence of concrete history the formation or genesis of what men have agreed to call philosophy.

In so doing we shall follow, so far as it is possible in an explanatory text-book, the actual method of Aristotle, too often neglected by books which teach his conclusions, but apparently ignore his spirit. That great realist advanced nothing *a priori* and always studied the historical development of a problem before he proposed his own solution, which thus appeared as the natural goal of a process of discovery. Such a method will no doubt compel us to undertake a considerable digression into the field of history, but it is, nevertheless, in our opinion indispensable.

On the one hand, from the practical and educational standpoint, an account of the historical origins of philosophic thought is the best method of acquainting beginners with the problems of philosophy, introducing them into the world, entirely new to them, of rational speculation, and furnishing them, incidentally, with much extremely useful knowledge. Their first requisite is to know what they are studying, and to possess a sufficiently live and accurate notion of the problems of philosophy presented in their simplest form.

On the other hand, in justice to our subject itself, to state straight away, with no previous examination or concrete justification, conclusions relating to the nature of philosophy, its object, dignity, and so forth, would be to present the traditional conception of philosophy under an arbitrary and *a priori* aspect wholly alien to it, and to risk enslaving our pupils to empty formulæ. By beginning, on the contrary, with a brief outline of the history of ancient philosophy up to Aristotle, that is to say until the conclusion of its formative period, we display philosophy in its origin and construction, and thereby show how the transition was effected between the teaching of common sense and the scientific knowledge of philosophers, how the great philosophic problems arose of themselves, and how a particular conception of philosophy, which will be put later to the test of discussion, results inevitably from this historical inquiry, and naturally forces itself upon the mind. We need not fear to insist upon these preliminary questions, which we shall have to consider again from another angle in criticism. They concern the very existence, the nature, and the value of philosophy.

PART ONE

THE NATURE OF PHILOSOPHY

I

PHILOSOPHIC THOUGHT BEFORE PHILOSOPHY IN THE STRICT SENSE

PHILOSOPHIC speculation, precisely because it is the supreme achievement of reason, is unknown to all the so-called primitive races. Indeed, even of the civilisations of antiquity the greater part either have possessed no philosophy or have failed to discover its true nature and distinctive character. In any case, philosophy only began to exist at a very late period about the eighth and especially the sixth century B.C., and then found the right path to truth by a success which must be regarded as extraordinary when we consider the multitude of wrong roads taken by so many philosophers and philosophic schools.

Nevertheless, some of the most elementary truths with which philosophy deals were known long before philosophy itself had come to birth, and the more important of these are to be found in a more or less rudimentary form and more or less seriously corrupted among all the peoples of antiquity, even at the most remote epochs. But it was not from the philosophers that these peoples had learned them ; their knowledge was derived in part from that wholly spontaneous and instinctive exercise of reason which we call common sense, but above all from primitive tradition.

23

The most reliable inductions of history combine with the conclusions of theology [1] to prove the existence of a *primitive tradition*, common to the different branches of the human race and going back to the origin of mankind. And even in default of any positive sources of information, it is a very reasonable conjecture that the first man received from God knowledge together with existence, that by education he might complete the work of procreation.

But was it possible that this knowledge, together with the primitive religion in which it was incorporated, could be transmitted in its integrity by the human race? We have, on the one hand, truths of the loftiest sublimity to be handed down from one generation to another, yet, on the other, an intelligence dominated by the senses and imagination. A disproportion so extreme inevitably deteriorated the tradition received at the outset, as little by little the rust of oblivion gathered upon it, error defiled it, and it fell a prey to the corruptions of polytheism and the more degraded forms of religion (animism, totemism, idolatry, magic, etc.). Nevertheless, in spite of the changes which it underwent, the primitive tradition has preserved for mankind throughout the ages a deposit, progressively diminishing no doubt, of fundamental truths. In this deposit were included many philosophic conceptions—that is to say, conceptions which concerned the most sublime problems within the scope of reason. But since they were taught only by a religious tradition which corroborated the instinctive teachings of common sense, they were

[1] P. Lemonnyer, O.P. (following Schmidt), *La Révélation primitive et les données actuelles de la science*. Paris, 1914.

known in a pre-philosophic fashion and existed in a pre-philosophic state.

It is not surprising that all peoples in the primitive[1] stage of history were ignorant of philosophic speculation. But it is more astonishing that even certain civilisations were devoid of philosophy—for example, the *Semitic*, and the *Egyptian*, which is, in this respect, in the same category as the Semitic. Despite the high level of scientific culture reached by the intellectual aristocracy of these races, the sole philosophic conceptions, it would seem, which the Egyptians and Chaldeans possessed were a few very general ideas, implicit in their religion, concerning the Deity, the human soul and its state after death, and the precepts of morality. These truths, which, moreover (as in the case of every race), are purer the further back we follow their history, were never made the subject of rational study and speculation, but were simply accepted, as also were their scientific beliefs, as part of a sacred tradition. Religion took the place of philosophy, and from religion these races received certain philosophic truths; philosophy they had none. In this matter the Jews did not differ from their fellow Semites. Scornful of human wisdom and the achievements of pure reason, and, indeed, without aptitude for such investigations, they produced no philosophers (at least not before Philo, who was a contemporary of

[1] Primitive in respect of a particular branch of the great human tree and so far as our knowledge of the past extends, but not primitive in the absolute sense. Far behind what we term the primitive state of the peoples known to us lies a long stretch of human history of which we know nothing.

Jesus Christ), but they possessed the prophets and the Law.

All the great *Indo-European* civilisations, on the other hand, manifest an impulse, which no doubt took widely different forms, towards rational and, in the strict sense, philosophic speculation. But, except in Greece (and to a very partial extent in India), this impulse nowhere succeeded in achieving an independent scientific discipline distinct from religion. A traditional religion did not in this case take the place of philosophy, but philosophy, or, we should rather say, human wisdom, penetrated religion and was confused with it. The wise man fulfilled a sacred function. He was not the head of a philosophic school, but the founder of a religious sect, if not of a new religion.

(*a*) Among the *Persians*,[1] whose original religion, so far as we know it from inscriptions, was a fairly pure *monotheism*, Zoroaster or Zarathustra founded Mazdeism or Zoroastrianism (about the eighth or sixth century B.C. ?), a powerful achievement of speculation which systematised (and incidentally distorted) certain fundamental truths derived from the primitive tradition,

[1] In this summary review of the great Aryan religions, we have been obliged not only to isolate by a process of abstraction the intellectual aspects of those religions with which the philosopher is concerned, but, moreover, to simplify considerably and reduce to an artificial classification doctrines whose vast and fluctuating complexity (this is especially true of Brahmanism and Buddhism), and occasional inconsistency, dismay historians. It should be added that the explanations of Oriental thought given by scholars are still largely conjectural and, in all probability, especially as far as philosophy is concerned, in many cases extremely inadequate.

in the attempt to give a rational explanation of the vast problem which has faced human thought from the outset, the problem of evil. By his failure to perceive that God is the sole supreme principle and the source of everything which exists, so far as it partakes of being, and that evil is mere privation of being without positive existence, and therefore that no creature is evil by nature, Zoroaster ended in *dualism* and taught the existence of two principles uncreated and co-eternal, the principle of Good (*Ormuzd*) and the principle of Evil (*Ahriman*), who share the dominion of the universe and whose unrelenting struggle constitutes its history. So far as Ahriman is to be identified with the rebel angel of primitive tradition, Zoroastrianism tended to make the devil a god striving against God.

(*b*) Among the peoples of *India*, whose intellectual and religious history is far more complex (since in this field no certainty has yet been reached, we present the interpretation of their beliefs which seems to us most probable), we witness a remarkable phenomenon. When the original religion—the primitive religion of the *Vedas*[1]—no longer proved sufficient to satisfy the intellectual demands or social needs of a more advanced civilisation, philosophic notions, which seem to have originated as interpretations of sacrifice and other sacred ritual, but developed in a spirit hostile to the ancient traditions and the cult of the

[1] The most ancient among the religious books of the Hindus (*Veda* means knowledge), the *Rig-Veda*, is apparently not older than the twelfth century B.C. Vedic religion seems to have been an incoherent polytheism coloured by a vague pantheism.

gods, found a home among the sacerdotal caste and took possession of the priesthood. To reconcile the perpetuation of their office with their new opinions, the priests, while continuing to perform the traditional ceremonies, directed their worship no longer to the old gods, but to the undefined and secret forces of the universe.

(i) This resulted, after a period of confusion, in the formation of a new system, *Brahmanism* (or Hinduism), which is essentially a philosophy, a metaphysic, a work of human speculation, but being, so to speak, clothed in the ornaments of the sanctuary, was invested from the outset with the sanctions and attributes of a religion. A divine origin was ascribed to the books in which it was taught (the *Brahmanas* and *Upanishads*), and they could be obtained only from the priests. Hence Brahmanism may be called a sacred, hieratic or theological metaphysic, and already in the eighth century B.C. the supremacy of the priestly caste among the Hindus seems to have realised in its fashion that social and spiritual sovereignty of the philosopher-priest and the religion of science which was the dream of certain nineteenth-century thinkers.

It is true that the science which those thinkers wished to invest with a sacred character was the science of phenomena, or, as it was termed, *positive science*, which is not wisdom, even human, and, as Auguste Comte justly observed, is incapable of producing order in any department. The human science to which Brahmanism gave a divine character was, on the contrary, the science of ultimate realities, *metaphysics*, human wisdom in the strict sense : a powerful effort of metaphysical thought (so far as we can judge of it from documents whose interpretation is still far from certain), but the product of reason still untrained, incapable of making the necessary distinctions and of avoiding internal contradictions, seduced by the dream of an intuitive knowledge of the All, angelic rather than human, and doomed by its very ambition.

This system, at least when we consider its predominant tendencies, taught that the First Principle of the world, named *Brahma* [1] or *Atman*, [2] constitutes in himself the intimate reality of everything which truly exists, whence logically follows *pantheism*, or the identification of God with his creation. [3] Nevertheless,

[1] From the name of the occult and sacred force which gave ritual its efficacy and pervaded all things. Originally regarded as the first emanation of the supreme God, it became for the Brahmans the unique source of being. The masculine noun, *Brahma*, designates the First Principle as God and Lord, the neuter, *Brahman*, as the one impersonal substance.

[2] From the name of the principle of life (the " self " transcending the phenomenal individual), which was regarded as animating man and the universe.

[3] The term *pantheism* is relatively recent, having been introduced into the vocabulary of philosophy by Toland in the eighteenth century. But the doctrine it designates is as ancient as the earliest philosophical errors.

For a system to be pantheistic, it need not explicitly identify God and creatures (very few pantheists fulfil this condition). It is sufficient that its teachings are logically irreconcilable with an absolute distinction between God and creatures.

This observation is particularly important for the study of Oriental philosophies, of which pantheism is the original sin. Indeed, it arises in their case from the very method of thought they employ, which appears to consist primarily in the treatment of analogous concepts (realised differently in different objects) as though they existed as such outside the mind, which led them to conclude that things which remain the same become on different planes of reality essentially different. For example, *Atman* is both the supreme principle of the universe, transcending all multiplicity, and the principle which distinguishes and constitutes every personality. Like the Schoolmen, but for

an attempt was made to avoid this conclusion. The Supreme Principle, which possesses neither personality nor knowledge, to which no attribute can be applied, which is absolutely unknowable by any concept, however universal, not even by the concept of being, so that it must be called Nothing or Non-Being, is the sole true reality. Therefore the existence of everything multiple or limited, everything we can know by our senses or even by our concepts, is as such illusion, mere appearance. This is *idealism*, the denial of the reality of the world and of things. But the bare existence of this appearance or illusion is an evil, indeed evil pure and simple. The existence of individual objects and of this cosmic delusion which is called Nature (Maya), and which keeps us captives of the manifold and the transitory, is essentially evil and the source of all suffering.

The problem of evil, therefore, seems to dominate the entire speculation of the Indian metaphysicians, as also of the Persian sages. But the Persians, whose bent was practical, always considered evil under the aspect of sin, and, obsessed with the differences between moral good and evil, which they attempted to use as a criterion to divide beings into two metaphysical categories, ended in dualism. The Hindus, on the

different reasons, the Indians distinguish between the personality (which is for us the spiritual subsistence of the soul) and the material individuality (which arises from the dispositions of the body).

This mode of thought, which we meet again more or less emphasized in every doctrine of *theosophic* orientation, makes it possible to avoid the appearance of pantheism, because its inherent self-contradiction permits the affirmation of essential differences between terms which should logically be identified. But, precisely because these affirmations are only possible in virtue of a fundamental self-contradiction, it inevitably involves a real pantheism.

contrary, exclusively occupied with contemplation, regarded evil pre-eminently under the aspect of suffering, or rather privation, in the sense in which metaphysicians understand the term.[1] Led astray by a profound realisation of a great truth which they were unable to apprehend clearly (for while it is very true that it were better for us not to exist than to exist without being united to God, they believed it were better for all things not to exist than to exist without being God), they ended in a pessimism which, though undoubtedly very different from the romantic pessimism of a Schopenhauer, was primarily the barren renunciation of a proud intellect, and attempted to be self-sufficient.

What, then, in their conception did wisdom teach man ? It taught him to free himself from suffering and illusion, and with that object to rid himself of all individual existence. The Brahmans held the doctrine of the transmigration of souls, or *metempsychosis* ; they believed that souls, on the death of the organism which

[1] From this point of view Indian speculation may be said to afford a prominent example of pure metaphysical intellectualism. Regarding things solely from the standpoint of intellectual speculation and the universal order, and not from the standpoint of the rectitude of the human will and that particular order by which man is ordered to his last end, it quickly came to lose sight almost entirely of the notion of moral good and evil, and its ethics consists primarily in a metaphysical purification, directed exclusively to a particular ideal of intellectual knowledge.

An analogous tendency is observable in every system which confuses by an exaggerated intellectualism the moral with the metaphysical order (a confusion which is glaring in Spinoza's *Ethics*, for example) and, failing to recognise that God is not only the *provisor universalis* of creation, but also the *provisor particularis* of the moral life (cf. St. Thomas, *Sum. Theol.* i, q. 103, a. 8, with Cajetan's *Commentary*), ends by claiming to transcend the distinction of good and evil and denying the existence of moral evil.

they had animated, passed into another organism, thus living successively in different bodies of men, animals, or plants.[1] The punishment of the wicked and foolish consisted accordingly in continuing to undergo in a series of reincarnations the pain of individual existence. The soul of the wise man, on the contrary, was delivered from the yoke of transmigration ; absorbed or reabsorbed in *Atman*, it escaped the sufferings of the world by losing all distinctive individuality.

The ethics of Brahmanism teaches the means whereby this deliverance can be achieved ; the wise man progresses towards that goal in this life by means of contemplation. Brahmanism understands that contemplation is a beginning of beatitude in this life ; but, as it mistakes the nature of beatitude, so it mistakes the nature of contemplation. The contemplation which it claims to teach is, in fact, only a metaphysical contemplation, or rather a species of supra-rational vision, which it expects to achieve by the merely natural powers of the created intellect ; unlike Christian contemplation, it is the product of the intellect alone, not of supernatural charity and the

[1] So, at least, metempsychosis is currently understood. It is not unlikely that this interpretation of the doctrine is the popular translation of a doctrine less crude, according to which every being passes through an indefinite series of states or cycles of existence, each of which is only lived once, and our earthly existence is simply one particular state among many others. If this be the case, the doctrine of successive reincarnations originated in an unintelligent distortion of this theory, still further corrupted when it was introduced into the West. (The possibility, however, remains that originally the Pythagoreans and Orphics understood the transmigration of souls in a symbolic sense.)

It is also possible, on the contrary, that the theory in question was a learned interpretation, elaborated by the Indian metaphysicians, of a popular belief in transmigration.

infused wisdom which accompanies it. Its aim is union with God by knowledge, not by love. Instead of admitting an activity overflowing from its own superabundance, it withdraws from activity of any kind, which it abandons wholly to the inferior powers. By this metaphysical contemplation, Brahmanism proposes to put us gradually in possession of our last end and initiate us into the blessed state of the delivered. Since it thus strives to reach by man's unaided powers heights which grace alone can attain, it results in a pseudo-mysticism of a purely intellectual character (in contrast to other, purely emotional, forms of false mysticism) in which the wise man, hoping not only to be united with God, but to blend with him, intoxicates himself not with God, but with his own self-annihilation. Hence (apart from those instances of genuine spirituality which grace is always free to produce) a host of counterfeits of supernatural mysticism, also of ascetic exercises and methods, including among their baser forms (with the fakirs) those *tours de force* of exaggerated asceticism which prove that the mortification of the flesh, when not regulated by reason and dictated by love, can be as fallacious as pleasure. *Naturalism* is thus the final characteristic and the capital vice of Brahmanism,[1] as indeed of philosophic mysticism in general, whether it be the product of Brahmanism, Buddhism, neo-Platonism, or Islam.

(ii) From the sixth century onwards new schools

---

[1] We do not mean that Brahmanism descends to the adoration of sensible nature, above which, on the contrary it claims to rise completely. By the term "naturalism" we here mean the claim to arrive at union with God and perfection without the supernatural assistance of grace.

arose in India, some orthodox, others heterodox. Of these the principal was that founded by Çakya-Muni, surnamed the Buddha [1] (the enlightened, the sage). *Buddhism,* a doctrine essentially negative and solvent, directed, moreover, to practice rather than to speculation, may be regarded as the corruption and dissolution of the Brahman philosophy.

Substituting for that which is that which passes away, refusing to say that anything does or does not exist, and admitting only a succession of impermanent forms without fixed foundation or absolute principle—in other words subordinating being to what is known as becoming or *fieri*—it showed, at the very time at which in Greece Heraclitus formulated the philosophy of flux, all the characteristics of a perfect evolutionary system, and, if it declared the existence of God, as of a substantial self and an immortal soul, unknowable (*agnosticism*), its real tendency was to deny the existence of God (*atheism*), and to substitute for substance of any kind a stream or flux, regarded indeed [2] as itself real, of forms or phenomena (phenomenalism).[3] Hence for Buddhism metempsychosis consists in a continuous chain of thoughts and feelings (a stream of consciousness, as we should term it to-day) passing from one mode of existence to another in virtue of a sort of urge towards life, due itself to the desire to live : it is desire which is the

[1] His actual name was Gautama. The name Çakya-Muni means the ascetic or hermit (*muni*) of the race or clan of the Çakya. Buddha lived during the second half of the sixth century B.C. He would seem to have died about the year 477.

[2] At least by Buddha's original disciples.

[3] " Everything is empty, everything unsubstantial " was a saying of Buddha's.

cause of existence and "we are what we have thought."

At the same time, the teaching of deliverance from suffering, which in Buddhism, even more than in Brahmanism, dominates the entire system, assumes a different and even more radical form. Evil is no longer merely the possession of individual or personal existence ; it is existence itself : it is evil to be, and the desire of existence is the root of all suffering. The wise man must therefore destroy in himself man's natural longing for existence and for beatitude, the fullness of being ; he must abandon all hope and extinguish every desire. He will thus attain the state of emptiness or total indetermination called *nirvana* (literally *nakedness*, metaphorically *immortality, refreshment, the farther bank*—the term, in itself indefinite, was never defined by Buddha), which will deliver him from the evil of existence and the yoke of transmigration, and which, in the logical consequence of Buddhist principles, must be regarded as the annihilation of the soul itself. For since the soul is only the chain or current of thoughts and feelings which derive their existence from the desire to be, to extinguish that desire is to extinguish the soul.

This *nirvana* is the goal for whose attainment Buddhism made use of the ascetic practices which it took over with considerable mitigation from Brahmanism, also of its moral code [1] which is thus directed, not to God, but to a species of mystical nothingness

[1] We here understand *moral code* in a very wide sense as meaning a code of behaviour. If the expression be taken as implying moral obligation, whose ultimate basis is the Christian doctrine of God the transcendent Creator, we must conclude that Buddhism, as indeed all the Oriental religions, Indian or Chinese, has no moral code.

as its last end. Moreover, the source and ultimate measure of Buddhist ethics is man, not God. If it rejected the system of castes which exaggerated the demands of social order and divided man almost into distinct species, it was only to dissolve social order of any kind in an absolute equality and individualism. And though it prescribed a universal benevolence (which extended even to prohibiting the slaughter of animals and to a compulsory vegetarianism), almsgiving, pardon of injuries, and non-resistance to the wicked, its motive was not love of one's neighbour as such, whose positive good and (by implication) existence we are bound to will, but to escape suffering to oneself by extinguishing all action and energy in a kind of humanitarian ecstasy. Buddhism is, therefore, a proof that gentleness and pity, when they are not regulated by reason and dictated by love, can deform human nature as much as violence, since they are then manifestations of cowardice, not of charity.

This doctrine of despair is not only a heresy from the point of view of Brahmanism ; it is an intellectual plague to humanity, because it proceeds from the negation of reason. It is not, therefore, surprising that we find in it the majority of the fundamental errors by which contemporary attacks on reason are inspired. If at the present day it has found a warm welcome among certain circles in Europe, it is because all those who hope to derive from humanitarianism a moral code of human kindness for the acceptance of an atheistic society are already implicitly Buddhists.

(iii) Buddhism is a philosophy, agnostic and atheistic, which nevertheless usurps the social and ritual functions of a religion. It is as a religion that it has won the allegiance of so many millions.[1] In certain other schools to which Brahmanism gave birth—schools recognised as " orthodox "—we find, on the other hand, a tendency towards the normal distinction between philosophy and religion.

These *darshanas*, it is true, would seem to be not so much distinct systems as complementary aspects of one and the same doctrine, the Brahmanist metaphysics. Here we may pass over the *Vedanta*, the most complete statement of that metaphysics and its doctrine of deliverance ; the *Mimamsa*, a species of commentary on the ritual and an explanation of the unseen forces set in motion by every act ; the *Sankhya*, founded, it is said, by Kapila (fifth or sixth century B.C. ?), which treats of the emanation of all things from their source, and seems to have taught, like Plato, a psychological dualism which explains suffering by the union souls contract with matter ; and also *Yoga*, which teaches the practical methods which lead to contemplation, that is to say, the total loss of consciousness and identification with the universal Being (*Ishvara*) by a supra-rational knowledge. But the *darshana Vaisesika*, ascribed to Kanada (about the fourth century B.C. ?), which includes a rough outline of cosmology, and divides everything which exists into a number of fundamental classes or categories, substance, quality, movement, association, difference, and

[1] However, in proportion as it has secured wide acceptance, Buddhism has ceased to be atheistic, only to fall into the most degraded conceptions of deity. Popular Buddhism as practised to-day in many parts of Asia, where, to adapt itself to existing beliefs, it has assumed the most varied shapes, is nothing more than a form of idolatry, totally different from philosophic Buddhism.

inherence, and explains the four elements of ponderable matter, earth, water, air, and fire, by the union of indivisible and indestructible particles, "atoms" in the language of philosophy,[1] and the *darshana Nyaya*, founded by Gotama, which attempts to construct a theory of reasoning and proof—that is to say a logic, though a logic extremely confused and incomplete— are clearly the rough sketches of a work strictly and solely philosophical. But these crude attempts did not lead to a completed system, and Indian thought never achieved a rational and autonomous philosophy.

(c) When we turn to the Far East and consider the very ancient civilisation of *China*,[2] we find that when the primitive religion of the Chinese, which seems to have been fairly pure,[3] had from the twelfth century B.C. undergone gross corruption and materialisation, substituting the sky for God,[4] worshipping the sun and moon, paying divine worship to the souls of ancestors and to spirits, and allowing itself to become tainted by magic and sorcery, wise men were compelled here

[1] Kanada, however, to explain this union, attributed real qualities to his atoms. Observe that Brahmanism, which rejects atomism, admits five elements (ether being the fifth) ; Buddhism on the contrary, which has welcomed atomism, only four.

[2] Whatever be the racial appurtenance of the Chinese, their history undoubtedly shows closer connections with the Aryans than with the Semites. It is for this reason that Chinese philosophy is discussed in the present section.

[3] It taught the existence of one sole God—*Shang-ti*—personal, intelligent, distinct from the world, Sovereign Ruler of the races of mankind ; also the immateriality and immortality of the human soul, and even offered to the spirits of ancestors the same sacrifices and marks of reverence as to the good spirits who are guardians of men.

[4] In all probability Heaven (*Tien*) was in origin simply a metaphorical synonym of the Sovereign Ruler (*Shang-ti*).

also to seek a remedy for a decadence which about the sixth century B.C. threatened their civilisation with utter ruin.

It has long been believed that the Chinese sages were simply moralists wholly occupied with laying down rules of conduct and completely indifferent to metaphysical speculation. This is a true account only of Confucius and his followers ; it does not seem to be applicable to Lao-Tse, though we can only accept with considerable reserve the interpretations of his teaching offered by certain modern Taoists.

According to their account, Lao-Tse (born 604 B.C.) was himself the disciple of a tradition whose oldest monument is the *Yi-King*, a book which consists essentially of sixty-four graphic symbols (hexagrams or double trigrams) arranged in a series of mechanical groups,[1] formed by combining simpler signs and susceptible of very many interpretations (metaphysical, logical, mathematical, moral, political, astronomic), each number corresponding analogically with the others. The metaphysical speculation of the *Yi-King* appears to have been primarily concerned with the question, How can the Absolute, being wholly self-sufficient, act and manifest itself? It distinguishes in the supreme and sole First Principle or Perfection two different aspects, *Chien*, the unmoving and unknowable source of all activity, and *Chuen*, knowable activity, which eternally manifests perfection in a process of spiral evolution and an endless flux of forms. But these two aspects merge in one single and self-identical being, and all things, after passing through all the forms

[1] Raymond Lull, in his attempts to create an ideographic algebra, employed an analogous procedure.

of evolution (of which the human cycle is but one curve), must return to *Chien*. This metaphysic may therefore be described as a species of *evolutionary pantheism*. It constitutes the foundation of Lao-Tse's system (Taoism), his chief contribution being an element of occultism and asceticism.[1] *Tao* (the Way), the eternal goal and process of evolution, is the road by which all things must pass to arrive finally at the complete cessation of activity (*Nibban*, the Chinese *nirvana*), in which they are reabsorbed in nothingness and become one with the first principle of all activity. The wise man will imitate the *Tao* by cutting himself off from all things, for the Way, though it has produced beings, does not partake of their movements. "Having built this house, it dwelleth not therein." Detached from wealth, passions, and sensible experience, and knowing that evil is mere appearance, he trains himself in solitude, secrecy, and humility (a humility which has nothing in common with the Christian virtue of that name, being nothing more than prudence and contempt for one's fellow men), until he reaches a state of perfect knowledge in which he no longer acts except by the pure intelligence. The wisdom, the illusory wisdom, to which Taoist asceticism leads its disciples, an asceticism which makes use of opium, as Buddhist asceticism of hypnosis, is for man a principle of revolt, therefore the adept

[1] It may be added that in the twelfth century A.D. Chu-Hi, who has been regarded, mistakenly it would seem, as a materialist, formulated, in the tradition of Lao-Tse, a system which in the Chinese system of education has become, practically speaking, the official philosophy. It explains the constitution of things by a dual principle (*li* and *ki*) which is not without resemblance to the duality of form and matter in Aristotle and the Alexandrians.

must keep it a secret for himself and a narrow circle of initiates.[1]

No doubt Confucius (Kung-fu-tse, 551–479 B.C.), who, unlike Lao-Tse, represents for the Chinese a moderate and practical wisdom (which, from its place in their system of education and its own active character, is generally accessible), preserved many truths of the primitive wisdom. He avoided, however, every ultimate question, and confined himself to an ethic purely human, social, earthly, and even commonplace. Opportunism, he observes, is the distinctive mark of the wise man. Every predetermined line of action, every preconception is a mistake. In all matters one should pursue a middle course, live unfettered by one fixed purpose, embrace no opinion with enthusiasm, reject nothing because it is antipathetic, do whatever seems best in the circumstances of the moment and as the situation demands. Confucianism, a system intended for the multitude, ended in pure materialism. Taoism, which claimed to address a small circle, and which, if the interpretation given above be correct, constitutes, together with Brahmanism, one of the most singular attempts ever made by man to attain, in that ignorance of love which seems an aboriginal characteristic of Oriental thought, a wisdom exclusively of the intellect, by which he could deify himself in metaphysics, has experienced in China alternate periods of triumph and persecution, and has organised, apparently ever since the opening centuries of our era, secret societies

[1] " Empty their heads, and fill their bellies," was Lao-Tse's advice to a statesman; " weaken their minds and strengthen their sinews. To teach the people is to ruin the State."

in which it has definitively taken refuge since the seventeenth century and in which it has degenerated into a philosophic and political occultism of the most pernicious type.

This brief historical sketch has shown the important part in the life of humanity played by sages and their wisdom. All these nations, situated on the frontiers of darkness, and lacking a divine revelation of truth, were obliged, when their religions proved incapable of satisfying the needs of the individual soul or of society, to have recourse to the wisdom supplied by human reason. This wisdom, in the civilisations of which we have spoken hitherto, was never differentiated from religion, but, on the contrary, encroached on the domain of the latter and claimed to conduct men to their last end, until in India we actually find that Brahmanism successfully achieved that canonisation of metaphysics which threatened the Greco-Roman world in the reign of the neo-Platonic emperor, Julian the Apostate. It achieved also that transfusion into religion of a human philosophy attempted by Kantian metaphysics in the nineteenth century (*Modernism*).

It has also shown how this human wisdom has everywhere proved bankrupt, and how, even before philosophy took shape as an independent discipline, most of the great philosophic errors had been already formulated. From the very first, the most arduous problems tower like mountains before the intellect of man ; the problem of evil, the problem of being, the problem of the becoming and flux of things. It is not, therefore, surprising that a reason liable to error the moment it transcended the elementary truths within the range of common sense, a reason still unstable and undisciplined, and therefore all the more ambitious, went astray from the outset and opened the history of metaphysics with the dualism of Zoroaster and the pessimism of the Hindu, the pantheism and idealism of the Brahmans, the atheistic evolutionism of Buddha, and the illusory wisdom of Lao-Tse. When it became more modest, it was only to fall into the ethical positivism of Confucius, renouncing all sublimity and even denying its own *raison d'être*. Nor should it surprise us to find the same errors reappearing at a later stage, when philosophy had been fully elaborated. Error, at whatever period of human history it may arise, is due to a failure of man's reasoning power—is, so to speak, a return of its primitive weakness, and therefore of its very nature retrograde.

A further fact, however, calls for remark here, a fact only too well established by this prehistory, so to term it, of philosophy : namely, that these fundamental errors are not unsubstantial and insignificant dangers ; they may succeed, to the bane of those diseased cultures which they condemn to sterility. Truth (in all matters which transcend the data of common sense) is not, as those are apt to believe who have had the good fortune to be born into a culture formed by it, given to man ready made, like a natural endowment. It is difficult to attain, and hard to keep, and only by a fortunate exception is it possessed uncontaminated by error and in the totality of its various complementary aspects. We have therefore the most urgent cause to be grateful for the possession of a revelation, by which God has given us from on high, besides a knowledge of supernatural truth inaccessible to reason, a sure and easy access to the essential elements of the same truth which, so far as it falls within the natural order, is indeed accessible to our speculation, but can be so easily missed by it. Those also have the strongest claim on our gratitude who from below, by the strenuous exercise of their reason and unaided by revelation, succeeded in bringing to light the principles and laying the permanent foundation of this natural truth, and in constructing a true and progressive human wisdom, in other words a philosophy, which, when met later and raised by the truth revealed from heaven, would be incorporated into the fabric of a higher wisdom, theology, the wisdom of man deified by grace, wisdom in the highest sense of the term. How highly therefore ought we to prize the sacred heritage of Greek thought !

In *Greece*, alone in the ancient world, the wisdom of man found the right path, and as the result of a fortunate harmony of the soul's powers and of a long effort to achieve mental order and discipline human reason attained its full vigour and maturity. In consequence, the small Hellenic race appears among the great empires of the East like a man amidst gigantic children, and may be truly termed the organ of the reason and word of man as the Jewish people was the organ of the revelation and word of God.

It was in Greece alone that philosophy achieved her autonomy and was explicitly distinguished from religion. At least during the purest and most glorious age of the Hellenic mind, it recognised its own boundaries and was content to claim a strictly limited territory—the scientific study of purely rational truths —whereas Greek religion, already very much degraded in the time of Homer, became increasingly incapable of satisfying the needs of the intelligence, and grew more corrupt every day. True, the time would come when the Greeks, arrogantly abusing philosophy and reason, would attempt to embrace the things of God within the limits of their wisdom, " would become vain in their thoughts " and deserve the condemnation pronounced by St. Paul on the wisdom of this world, " which is foolishness in the sight of God." But their philosophy, though born of their mind, is undefiled by their corruptions, and its sole object is the truth.

II

THE PRE-SOCRATIC PHILOSOPHERS

THE earliest thinkers of Hellas were the poets, the interpreters of traditional religion. Myth-makers, like Hesiod or Homer, sometimes prophets, such as that Epimenides of Cnossos who purified Athens from pestilence by erecting altars to unnamed divinities, they have no place in the history of philosophy in the strict sense. Greek philosophy, as Aristotle shows, only began with Thales of Miletus, one of the *Sages* or Gnomics, who lived in the seventh or sixth centuries B.C.[1]

The primary aim of these Sages, traditionally seven in number (their names are variously handed down by ancient writers), was to improve the conduct of their fellow citizens. Their aphorisms, some of which Plato quotes in the *Protagoras*, do no more than embody the practical lessons they had learned from their experience of life. They were men of action, legislators, or moralists, men of prudence, but not yet philosophers. Alone among them Thales embarked on scientific speculation. Geometrician and astronomer, he demonstrated that all the angles inscribed in a semicircle are right angles, and appears to have predicted—no doubt owing to his acquaintance with

[1] For the fragments from the early philosophers quoted in this chapter Professor Burnet's translation (*Early Greek Philosophy*) has been used ; for Aristotle's *Metaphysics* Professor W. D. Ross's translation.

Babylonian science—the total eclipse of the sun which occurred on May 28th, 585.

The philosophers who succeeded him were still for the most part men who played an active part in public affairs, ardent politicians of the city state ; but, in spite of this practical activity, they were more or less clearly conscious from the beginning of the true nature of their wisdom. Moreover, save in the case of a few exceptional individuals (for instance, Empedocles, the miracle worker, and Pythagoras, who founded a religious sect), Greek philosophy was from the very first distinct from religion—indeed it took shape as a critic and foe of the popular mythology and was manifestly the product of pure reasoning.

In this work we are concerned only with the progressive development of Greek philosophy from Thales to Aristotle, for it was during this period that philosophy, with its absolute validity for mankind as a whole, took definite shape. The process occupied some three centuries and is divisible into three great epochs—the period of formation (the pre-Socratic philosophers), the period of crisis (the Sophists and Socrates), the period of fruitful maturity (Plato and Aristotle).

THE IONIANS

(a) Human reason now set out with its unaided powers in search of the principles and causes of things. What first strikes man's intelligence is what he sees and touches, what he knows by his senses, and when he attempts to understand anything, he begins by asking what it is made of. Therefore the first thinkers of Hellas only considered in things the material of which they are made, their matter (what we shall learn to call the *material cause*), which they naively took to be a complete explanation of the object. Moreover, since the most universal and most important phenomenon of nature is change, especially the change by which one body becomes another (*e.g.* bread becomes flesh, wood fire), they concluded that the original matter of which all things are fashioned must be identical in all, the common subject of all corporeal changes. But since they were still unable to conceive any impalpable or invisible principle, they thought they had discovered this matter in some one of the elements perceived by the senses.

Thales, for example (624–546), influenced by traditional myths which derived all things from the primordial waters, and arguing from the fact that plants and animals " are nourished by moisture " and that the germ of animal life is moist, concluded that *water* is the sole substance, preserving its identity through all the transformations of bodies. For Anaximenes (588–524) this substance was *air*, for Heraclitus (540–475 ?) *fire*, for Anaximander (610–547) the *boundless* (by which he understood the *indeterminate*, ἄπειρον), a fusion of all the contraries. Moreover, water, air, fire, and the boundless were regarded as something active, living, and animate, endowed by an internal force with a manifold and unlimited fecundity. This was the meaning of Thales's dictum, all things " are full of gods," πάντα πλήρη θεῶν.[1] From the history of this extremely primitive Ionian school, whose philosophy is termed *hylozoist* because it ascribed life (ζωή) to matter (ὕλη), we learn

[1] Aristotle, *De Anima*, i, 5, 411 a 7.

to regard as the most elementary and crude of philosophic doctrines the *materialistic monism* which teaches the existence of a one single substance of a material nature, and *evolutionism*, which attempts to explain everything by an historic process of unfolding, development, or evolution of something pre-existent.

Evolutionism, which, owing, on the one hand, to German metaphysics, on the other to Darwin and Spencer, became so popular in the nineteenth century, was already taught in Greece by the physicists of the sixth and fifth centuries B.C.[1] Anaximander in particular taught the eternal evolution of worlds " which rise and set at long intervals," and held that animals sprang from the mud of the sea floor, clothed at first, as with a species of shell, in a prickly bark which they shed on dry land,[2] and that man arose from animals of another species,[3] having been originally formed within the bodies of fishes, where he developed, being ejected as soon as he had become sufficiently large to provide for himself.[4]

Later *Empedocles* of Agrigentum (493–433 ?), whose speculation in other respects marks an advance on that of the Ionians,[5] explained the origin of living beings

[1] In India about the same date Buddhism was formulating, as we have seen, the religion of evolutionism.

[2] *Plac. Philos.*, v, 19, 1. Dox. 430, 15.

[3] Pseudo-Plut., *Strom.*, frag. 2, Dox. 579, 17.

[4] Plut., *Symp.*, q. viii. 579, 17.

[5] For a single corporeal substance Empedocles substituted four elements specifically different, the four which became later the four classical elements of ancient chemistry—earth, water, air, fire. His dominant interest was to discover the efficient cause of the evolution of things, which he believed to consist in the two great motive forces love and hate. Empedocles was not only a philosopher : he was also a magician, doctor, poet, orator, and statesman. Aristotle ascribes to him the invention of rhetoric.

by the separate production of the individual organs and members, *e.g.* the head, eyes, arms, which were subsequently joined by chance in every possible combination, of which only those have survived which were fitted to live (*cf.* the Darwinian principle of the survival of the fittest).

It is also worth remark that, before Democritus, Anaximander and Empedocles also sought, like the pseudo-scientific evolutionism of modern times, to explain all things *mechanically*, that is to say—as the result of a simple aggregation of material elements effected by local motion.

(*b*) Among these *physicists*, as Aristotle termed them, or philosophers of sensible nature, must be reckoned three great thinkers, Heraclitus, Democritus, and Anaxagoras.

(i) *Heraclitus* of Ephesus,[1] a lonely and proud genius who despised the multitude and popular religion, drew heroically from the thought of the Ionian philosophers its ultimate metaphysical presuppositions, and thereby fixed for all succeeding ages one of the possible extremes of speculation and error. A particular reality perceived in things had taken hold of his intellect with such force that he became its hopeless slave. That reality was *change* or *becoming*. His vision was so fixed on the change which all things undergo that he declared that change alone is real. Πάντα ῥεῖ, all things are in flux ; and men are fools to trust in the stability of their false happiness, " when they are born, they wish to live and to meet their

[1] The dates of Heraclitus's birth and death are uncertain. He was in his ἀκμή the prime of his age, about 500 B.C.

doom—or rather to rest—and they leave children behind them to meet their doom in turn." We do not touch the same thing twice nor bathe twice in the same river. The very moment we touch an object, it has already ceased to be what it was before. Whatever exists changes from the very fact of its existence.

That is to say change has no abiding and permanent subject identical with itself, like an ivory billiard ball which remains an ivory billiard ball while it is in motion. We are therefore compelled to pronounce boldly that that which is (the thing which changes) at the same time is not (because there is nothing which persists throughout the change). " We step and do not step into the same river ; we are and are not." Moreover, contraries must be pronounced identical. The sea is the purest and the impurest water. Good and ill are one. " No one," writes Aristotle in a famous passage, " can possibly conceive that the same thing does and does not exist. According to some, Heraclitus was of a different opinion, but we are not obliged to believe that a man really thinks whatever he says. The reason of the opinion held by these philosophers was that the only realities they admitted were sensible objects, and, since they perceived that sensible nature is in perpetual motion, some have held with Cratylus [1] that no statement can be made about it ; he was content to wag his finger." [2] This scepticism was the inevitable consequence of Heraclitus's philosophy of pure flux, despite his personal conviction,

[1] One of Heraclitus's most famous disciples. He was Plato's first teacher. (Aristotle, *Metaph.*, i, 6.)
[2] *Metaph.*, iv, 5, 1010 a 13.

passionately held, of the reality and value of truth. " If you do not expect the unexpected," he said, " you will not find truth, for it is hard to be sought out and difficult."

Heraclitus is thus the philosopher of evolution and becoming. In his view, all things are differentiations produced by discord or strife (πόλεμος πατὴρ πάντων) of a single mobile principle which he conceives in the form of fire, a fire ethereal, living, and divine. So from the outset stands out in the clearest light that fatal necessity which chains every philosophy of pure becoming to *monism*[1] or to *pantheism*.[2] " If," wrote Aristotle,[3] " you maintain that all beings are one, you simply return to Heraclitus's opinion. All things are then confused, good and evil become identical, man and the horse are one and the same thing. But this is really to maintain not that beings are one, but that they are nothing."

(ii) Born within a few years of Heraclitus's death, *Democritus* of Abdera (470–361 ?), who had a more superficial intellect and a predilection for ideas easily comprehensible, attempted to discover in the flux of sensible phenomena a permanent and unchanging element ; but in his search for this unchanging element he made use of his imagination rather than his understanding. Therefore the sole reality he would recognise was something which, though it is inaccessible to the senses, can nevertheless be apprehended by the imagination—namely, pure geometrical quantity as such, stripped of all qualities (colourless,

---

[1] The doctrine that all things are one single being.
[2] The doctrine which identifies the world with God.
[3] *Phys.*, i, 2, 185 b 19.

scentless, tasteless, etc.), and possessed solely of extension in the three dimensions of space. Democritus found the explanation of everything in the *plenum*, which he identified with being, and the *void*, identified with nonentity. The *plenum* was divided into indivisible parts of extension (" atoms "), which were separated one from another by the void and in a state of everlasting motion, and differed only in shape,[1] order,[2] and position.[3] The order of the universe and the structure of individual beings he attributed to the blind necessity of chance. Thus Democritus [4] introduced into Greek philosophy during the lifetime of Socrates the doctrine of *atomism* and more generally the philosophy termed *mechanical*, which raises geometry to the position of metaphysics, reduces everything to extension and motion, and professes to explain the organisation of the universe by a host of fortuitous coincidences. In this fashion the Parthenon could be " explained " as the result of throwing stones one on another during an indefinite term of

[1] As, for example, A differs from N.

[2] As AN differs from NA.

[3] As N differs from the same letter placed differently : Z.

[4] As also his master Leucippus. Had Leucippus and Democritus come in any way under the influence of the Indian philosopher Kanada? The more likely hypothesis is a coincidence due to similarity of intellectual outlook, particularly if Kanada, whose date is very uncertain, was contemporary with or even posterior to Democritus. Speaking generally, there seems no reason to believe that Oriental speculation so influenced Greek thought as to teach it in the strict sense or transmit any particular system. That, on the other hand, it influenced the Greeks by arousing a spirit of speculative inquiry and providing intellectual material (which they alone were able to treat scientifically) is the obvious conclusion from the simple fact that Greek philosophy originated in those provinces of the Hellenic world which were in contact with the East.

years, the tragedies of Racine as due to the indiscriminate shuffling of type for a sufficient length of time.

(iii) Finally *Anaxagoras* of Clazomenae (500–428), who was a friend of Pericles, and in the maturity of his powers when Democritus was born and Heraclitus had just died, turned Greek philosophy towards a higher source of illumination, and corrected rather than continued the speculation of the Ionians by the aid of ideas which, it must be confessed, he either worked out badly or was unable to use.

On the one hand, he perceived that the material principle of which all bodies are formed, and which the Ionians had identified with one particular element, must already somehow contain in itself the entire diversity to which it will give birth : unless everything were in everything, nothing could come from nothing.[1] He therefore concluded that the principle in question consisted of an endless mixture of all natures and qualities in such fashion that each corporeal particle contained within itself the elements (*homoeomeries*) of all the rest ; for example, each particle of the bread we eat contains invisible elements of the bone, blood, flesh, etc., which will be discovered later, changed only in their relative proportions, in each particle of bone, blood, flesh, etc. It was a bizarre conception, and, as taught by Anaxagoras, not worth serious discussion, but nevertheless a crude adumbration of Aristotle's great conception of *first matter* (*materia prima*) which is nothing *in act*, but all bodies *in potentiality*.

[1] *Cf.* Aristotle, *Phys.*, i, 4, 187 a 26. Simplicius, *Phys.*, 155, 23.

On the other hand—and it is his chief claim to distinction—he realised that the material principle, that of which all things are made, is insufficient to explain them. We must also discover the agent that produces them (the *efficient* or motor *cause*) and the end for which the agent acts (the *final cause*). Is it, as Plato was to ask later, a sufficient explanation of the fact that Socrates is sitting in prison to say that he has bone, joints, and muscles arranged in a particular fashion? We must also know who brought about that disposition of these bones and muscles—namely, Socrates himself by his will—and why he willed it.

Because Anaxagoras arrived at the recognition that there must necessarily exist, besides the material elements of the world, a separate Intelligence (νοῦς) to which the ordering of the universe is due, he alone, as Aristotle remarks " kept sober " when all the other philosophers of his period, drunk with the wine of sensible appearances, " spoke at random." [1]

THE ITALIANS

Besides the school of Ionian philosophy, there existed in the Hellenic world of the sixth and fifth centuries B.C. two other great philosophic schools— the Pythagorean and the Eleatic.

Pythagoras of Samos (572–500 ; according to other authorities, 582–497), the founder of a philosophic society of a religious and political character, which held the reins of government in several cities of Magna Graecia (Southern Italy), and was later dissolved by

[1] *Metaph.*, i, 3, 984 b 18.

violence,[1] understood that there existed realities of a higher order than those perceptible by the senses. But it was by the study of *numbers* that he had arrived at the knowledge of these invisible realities, whose immutable order dominated and determined the process of becoming ; and henceforward he had understanding only for numbers. Not content with teaching that there is present in all objects and in the universe as a whole a hidden principle of measure and harmony, he taught that numbers—by which this harmony is revealed to our senses—are the sole true reality, and regarded them as the very essence of things. Pythagoras was not only conversant with the important observations of Oriental astronomy, but, by his fundamental discovery of the relationship between the pitch of sounds and the length of vibrating strings, had reduced to the rigidity of numerical law so fugitive a phenomenon as sound. Imagine the awed astonishment with which he must have discovered behind the flux of sensible phenomena the intelligible constant and immaterial proportions which explain to the mathematician the regularities we observe. Consider, moreover, the mysterious symbolic value of numbers attested alike by the sacred traditions of mankind and the most positive of philosophers (from Aristotle, who paid homage to the holiness of the number 3, to Auguste Comte, who will construct an entire mythology of the prime numbers), and it is easy to understand how naturally the thought of Pythagoras

---

[1] In this society absolute obedience prevailed even in the speculative sphere. It was in the Pythagorean brotherhood, not in the schools of the Christian Middle Ages, that everything yielded to the *Magister dixit*, αὐτὸς ἔφα

and his disciples passed from the sign to the cause and made the symbol a principle of reality.

Consequently, numerical principles were regarded as the principles of everything that exists ; from the opposition between the determinate and the indeterminate (infinite) are derived all the fundamental pairs of opposites—odd and even, the elements of number, the one and the many, right and left, male and female, rest and motion, straight and crooked, light and darkness, good and evil, the square and the quadrilateral with unequal sides—which determine the nature and activity of things. Every essence has its number and every essence is a number. The number 4, for example, is not simply a figure of justice, it constitutes the essence of justice ; similarly the number 3 constitutes holiness, the number 7 time, the number 8 harmony, the number 5 the union of the sexes, the number 10 perfection. When numbers which in themselves are not localised receive a position in space, bodies come into existence. Thus all speculation on the origin or nature of things resolves itself into speculation on the genesis and properties of numbers.

Pythagoras, therefore, and his school, to whom mathematics, music and astronomy owe so much, never arrived at the true conception of the first philosophy or metaphysics. They achieved, it is true, a degree of abstraction superior to that at which the Ionians had halted, and did not, like them, confuse metaphysics with physics. But they confused it with the science of number, into which, moreover, they imported qualitative interpretations ; and, consequently, in spite of their effort to reach the object of pure intelligence, they were held fast in the bonds of imagination. And if, on the other hand, they perceived that the nature of things is intrinsically determined by immaterial principles more real and truer than that which is tangible and visible, they were not yet able to attain the notion of the *formal cause*, whose full elucidation was reserved to Aristotle alone.

It is to Pythagoras, as we have already remarked, that we owe the term *philosophy*. A passage of Diogenes Laertius (viii, 8) shows that for him the dignity of science consisted in its purely speculative and disinterested character, a point on which Aristotle, at the beginning of his *Metaphysics*, was to insist strongly. " Human life," he said, " may be compared to the public games, which attract diverse sorts of men. Some come to compete for honours and the crowns of victory, others to trade, others, the more noble sort, solely for the enjoyment of the spectacle. Similarly in life some work for honour, others for profit, a few for truth alone ; they are the philosophers. . . ." Pythagoras appears to have taught the unity of God, whom he regarded as one omnipresent Spirit from whom our spirits emanated. He was the first to give the universe the name κόσμος, which, like the Latin *mundus*, conveys the idea of *beauty* and *harmony*.

The most famous and the most derided of his tenets was the doctrine of the transmigration of souls, or *metempsychosis*, which he probably derived not from Egypt, as Herodotus suggests, but from Hinduism (by way of Persia) ; [1] a doctrine which very early

[1] As Gomperz observes, " the Asiatic Greeks and a portion of the population of India were already subject, when Pythagoras left his

obtained in Greece the adhesion of the Orphics and the Pythagoreans. " Coming one day upon a puppy which was being cruelly beaten," the aged Xenophanes wrote of Pythagoras in mordant verse, " he lamented its fate and cried out in pity ' Stop ! Don't beat him. That is the soul of one of my friends ; I recognise him by his voice.' "

The Pythagoreans also believed that the revolution of cosmic cycles must produce the everlasting recurrence at enormous intervals of all things, reproduced identically even in the most insignificant details. " According to the Pythagoreans," Eudemus told his disciples, " a day will come when you will be all gathered again, sitting in the very same places to listen, and I shall be telling you the same story once more." [1]

Astronomy was among the sciences which the Pythagorean school cultivated most successfully. Philolaus, who taught that the earth, the sun, and all the stars revolved around a mysterious centre of the universe filled with fire, may be regarded as a distant precursor of Copernicus. But even in this sphere the Pythagoreans betrayed in the most flagrant fashion the vices of the exclusively mathematical mind.

native Ionia, to the same ruler, Cyrus, the founder of the Persian Empire " (*Thinkers of Greece*, i, 3).

Speaking more generally, it was, it would appear, by way of the Pythagorean school that certain distinctively Oriental conceptions and modes of thought first entered Greece, to pass from Pythagoreanism to Platonism and neo-Platonism, and thence, swollen by further additions, into Gnosticism and the more or less underground stream of heterodox speculation.

[1] Simplicius, *Phys.*, 732, 30 D. Nietzsche, who was obsessed and driven to despair by the thought " of the everlasting recurrence of things," derived this singular conception from Greek philosophy.

" The Pythagoreans," wrote Aristotle,[1] " having been brought up in the study of mathematics . . . suppose the whole heaven to be a musical scale and a number. All the properties of numbers and scales which they could show to agree with the attributes and parts, and the whole arrangement of the heavens, they collected and fitted into their scheme ; if there was a gap anywhere, they readily made additions so as to make their whole theory coherent. For example, as the number 10 is thought to be perfect and to comprise the whole nature of numbers, they say that the bodies which move through the heavens are ten ; but as the visible bodies are only nine, to meet this they invent a tenth—the counter-earth—not studying the phenomena to discover their causes and test their hypotheses, but imposing upon the phenomena their hypotheses and preconceived beliefs, thereby claiming to assist God to fashion the universe."

THE ELEATICS

Though it cannot, strictly speaking, be said that the school of Elea founded metaphysics, since it failed to keep a firm grasp of the truth, it must receive the credit of having raised Greek thought to the metaphysical level and attained the necessary degree of abstraction. The oldest of the Eleatics was Xenophanes, a wandering rhapsodist, born about the year 570 at Colophon, whence he migrated to Elea in southern Italy—banished, no doubt, by the Persian invasions. Xenophanes poured scorn upon the mythology of the poets and the opinions of the common

[1] *Metaph.*, i, 5, 986 a. *De Caelo*, ii, 13, 293 a.

people. "Far better," he said, in slighting reference
to the honours paid to athletes, "is our art than the
strength of men and horses." He taught the absolute
unity of God, but confounded him with the universe,
declaring in a pantheistic sense that God is one and
all, ἓν καὶ πᾶν.

But the most profound thinker, indeed the true
founder of this school, was his disciple *Parmenides* of
Elea (born 540), the Great Parmenides, as Plato
called him. Transcending the world of sensible
phenomena and even that of mathematical forms or
essences and numbers, he attained to that in things
which is purely and strictly the object of the intellect.
For it can scarcely be denied that the first truth about
things which the intellect perceives is that they exist,
their being. The notion of being, thus abstracted,
impressed Parmenides so powerfully that it fascinated
him. As his contemporary Heraclitus was the slave
of *change*, Parmenides was the slave of *being*. He
had eyes for one thing alone : what is is, and cannot
not be ; being is, non-being is not. Parmenides was
thus the first philosopher who abstracted and formulated the principle of *identity* or non-contradiction, the
first principle of all thought.

And as he contemplated pure being, he perceived
that this being is completely one, absolute, immutable,
eternal, without becoming, incorruptible, indivisible,
whole and entire in its unity, in everything equal to
itself, infinite [1] and containing in itself every perfection. [2] But while he thus discovered the attributes of
him who is, he refused to admit that any other being

---

[1] Simplicius, *Phys.*, 144, 25 – 145, 23. (Diels, frag. 8, 22.)
[2] Aristotle, *Phys.*, i, 3.

could exist, and rejected as a scandal to the reason the being mingled with non-entity, because produced from nothingness, of every creature.

He was thus led so far astray that he ascribed to the being of the world that which belongs only to uncreated being. And rather than be false to what he believed were the exigencies of being and reason, he preferred to refuse heroically the witness of the senses and deny the existence in the universe of change or multiplicity. Change, motion, becoming, as also the diversity of things, are but an illusory appearance. There exists only being, the one.

Does not change imply that an object both was and was not (what it becomes), and at the same time continues and ceases to be (what it was) ? Does not multiplicity imply that what is (this) is not (that) ? Do not, therefore, multiplicity and change contradict the fundamental principle that what is possesses in itself being and not non-being ?

It was in defence of Parmenides's doctrine of the impossibility of change that his disciple Zeno of Elea [1] (born 487) composed his famous arguments, by which he claimed to prove that the very concept of movement is self-contradictory : arguments fallacious, no doubt, but of singular force and refutable only by the doctrine of Aristotle.

Thus Parmenides, reaching the opposite pole to Heraclitus, fixed, as he did, once for all one of the extreme limits of speculation and error, and proved that every philosophy of pure being, for the very reason that it denies that kind of non-being which

[1] Not to be confused with Zeno the Stoic, who lived much later (350–264) and was born at Cittium in Cyprus.

Aristotle termed *potentiality* and which necessarily belongs to everything created, is obliged to absorb all being in absolute being, and leads therefore to monism or pantheism no less inevitably than the philosophy of pure becoming.

III

THE SOPHISTS AND SOCRATES

THE long effort of these speculative pioneers which we have briefly recapitulated had equipped human thought with a number of fundamental truths. But if, looking backwards with a knowledge of the mighty synthesis in which all those truths, then partially perceived, have been harmonised and balanced, we can contemplate with admiration the gradual formation of the vital centres and arteries of philosophy, at the time, in fifth-century Hellas, these good results were concealed not only by the medley of contradictory theories, but by the number and gravity of prevalent errors, and it seemed as though the entire movement had achieved nothing but disorder and chaos.

The Greek thinkers had set out with high hopes of knowing everything, and climbing the sky of wisdom in a single step. As a result of this immoderate ambition, and because they lacked discipline and restraint in handling ideas, their concepts were embroiled in a confused strife, an interminable battle of opposing probabilities. The immediate and obvious result of these attempts at philosophising seemed the bankruptcy of speculative thought. It is not, therefore, surprising that this period of elaboration produced a crisis in the history of thought, at which an intellectual disease imperilled the very existence of philosophic speculation. This intellectual disease was sophistry, that is to say, the corruption of philosophy.

THE SOPHISTS

Sophistry is not a system of ideas, but a vicious attitude of the mind. Superficially the sophists were the successors and disciples of the thinkers of an earlier generation—even the word *sophist* originally bore no derogatory significance—in reality they differed from them completely. For the aim and rule of their knowledge was no longer that which is, that is to say, the *object* of knowledge, but the interest of the knowing *subject*.

At once wandering professors accumulating honours and wealth, lecturers, teachers of every branch of learning, journalists, if one may so call them, supermen, or dilettanti, the sophists were anything in the world but wise men. Hippias, who achieved equal eminence in astronomy, geometry, arithmetic, phonetics, prosody, music, painting, ethnology, mnemotechnics, epic poetry, tragedy, epigram, dithyramb, and moral exhortation, ambassador of Elis, and jack-of-all-trades (he attended the Olympic Games in clothes made entirely by himself), reminds us of some hero of the Italian Renaissance. Others resemble the *philosophes* of the eighteenth or the " scientists " of the nineteenth century. But the most characteristic feature of all alike was that they sought the advantages conferred by knowledge without seeking truth.

They sought the advantages conferred by knowledge so far as knowledge brings its possessor power, pre-eminence, or intellectual pleasure. With this in view, they put themselves forward as rationalists and walking encyclopaedias; to every question they had an answer ready, deceptively convincing;[1] and they claimed to reform everything, even the rules of grammar and the gender of nouns.[2] But their favourite study was man, of all the most complex and uncertain, but one in which knowledge is easiest coined into power and reputation; and they cultivated most assiduously law, history, casuistry,[3] politics, and rhetoric. They professed to be teachers of virtue.

They did not seek truth. Since the sole aim of their intellectual activity was to convince themselves and others of their own superiority, they inevitably came to consider as the most desirable form of knowledge the art of refuting and disproving by skilful arguments, for with men and children alike destruction is the easiest method of displaying their strength, and the art of arguing with equal probability the pros and cons of every question—another proof of acumen and skill. That is to say, in their hands knowledge altogether lost sight of its true purpose, and what with their predecessors was simply a lack of intellectual discipline became with them the deliberate intention to employ concepts without the least regard for that delicate precision which they demand, but for the pure

[1] Critias, for example, considered belief in the gods as the invention of an astute statesman who sought to keep the citizens obedient by clothing the truth in a garment of fiction.

[2] It was Protagoras who attempted to rationalise the genders of nouns: desiring, for example, that μῆνις (anger) should be given the masculine gender, also πήληξ (helmet), etc.

[3] Recall, for example, the celebrated discussion between Protagoras and Pericles after an accidental homicide in the course of an athletic contest, on the question who ought to be punished: the man who arranged the contest, the unskilful player, or the javelin itself.

pleasure of playing them off one against the other—
an intellectual game of conceptual counters devoid
of solid significance. Hence their *sophisms* or quibbles.
Their ethics were of a piece. Every law imposed
upon man they declared to be an arbitrary convention,
and the virtue they taught was in the last resort either
the art of success, or what our modern Nietzscheans
call *the will to power*.

Thus, of the spirit which had inspired the lofty
intellectual ambitions of the preceding age, the sophists
retained only the pride of knowledge ; the love of
truth they had lost. More ardently than their predecessors they desired to achieve greatness through
knowledge, but they no longer sought reality. If we
may use the expression, they believed in knowledge
without believing in truth. A similar phenomenon
has recurred since in the history of thought and on a
far larger scale.

Under these conditions the sole conclusion which
sophism could reach was what is termed *relativism* or
scepticism. Protagoras of Abdera (480–410), for example, maintained that " man is the measure of all
things—of what is, that it is, and of what is not, that
it is not," by which he meant that everything is
relative to the dispositions of the subject and the
truth is what appears true to the individual. And his
contemporary, Gorgias of Leontini (died 375), a famous
orator, in his book entitled *Of Nature or the Non-
Existent*, taught (i) that being is not, in other words,
that nothing exists : non-existence is non-existence,
and therefore it *is*—a quibble on the word *is* which
one day would be Hegel's grand metaphysical game—
hence being, its contrary, is not ; (ii) that if anything

67

existed we could not know it ; (iii) that if anyone could know anything, he could not communicate his knowledge to another.

SOCRATES

It was *Socrates* (469–399) who saved Greek thought from the mortal danger into which the sophists had brought it. Except for the fact that he took no fees for his instruction, his manner of life was externally the same as theirs. Like them, he spent his time in discussions with young men, and it is not surprising that a superficial observer, such as Aristophanes, confused him with the sophists. In reality, he waged against them an unrelenting war and opposed them at every point. The sophists claimed to know everything and did not believe in truth ; Socrates professed ignorance and taught his hearers to seek nothing but the truth. Thus his entire work was a work of conversion. He reformed philosophic reasoning and directed it to the truth, which is its proper goal.

This work was of such importance for the future of the human intellect that it is not strange that Socrates accomplished it as a mission divinely imposed. He possessed not only an extraordinary power of philosophic contemplation (we are informed by Aulus Gellius and Plato that he sometimes passed entire days and nights motionless, absorbed in meditation) but also something which he himself regarded as *daimonic* or inspired, a winged fervour, a free but measured force, even perhaps at times an interior instinct of a higher order, gifts suggestive of that extraordinary assistance in regard to which Aristotle said that those who are moved by a divine impulse need no guidance of human reason, since they possess in themselves a better principle.[1] He compared himself to a gadfly sent to sting the Athenians awake and force upon their reason a constant examination of conscience, a service which they repaid with hemlock, thus affording the aged Socrates, already on the verge of the grave, opportunity for the most sublime death to which merely human wisdom can lead.

(a) Socrates was not a metaphysician, but a practitioner, a physician of souls. His business was not to construct a system, but to make men think. This was the method by which he could best conquer a sophistry whose radical vice was not so much an error of doctrine as a deformity of the soul.

For the chief topic of Socrates's discussions was the problem of the conduct of human life, the moral problem. His *ethics*, as far as we can judge it by the reports of Plato and Xenophon, seems at first sight to have been dictated by narrowly utilitarian motives. What I ought to do is what is good for me, and what is good for me is what is useful to me—really useful. But at once the need becomes evident of discovering what is really useful to man ; and at this point Socrates compelled his hearers to acknowledge that man's true utility can only be determined by reference to a good, absolute, and incorruptible. By thus constantly raising the question of man's last end,[2] and directing men towards their sovereign good, he went beyond utilitarianism of every description, and,

[1] *Magn. Moral.*, vii, 8. *Cf. Eth.*, vii, 1.
[2] A question which he himself seems to have answered somewhat ambiguously.

69

with the full force of a sane common sense, vindicated the supremacy of moral good and our great eternal interests ; his ethics thus passed over into the metaphysical sphere. In the second place Socrates proved by every method of argument that in order to behave rightly man's first requisite is *knowledge* ; he even went so far as to maintain that virtue is identical with knowledge and therefore that the sinner is simply an ignorant man. Whatever we think of this mistake, the fact remains that for Socrates ethics was nothing if not a collection of truths established by demonstration, a real and a genuine science. In this twofold character, metaphysical and scientific, of his moral teaching, he stood in radical opposition to the sophists, and may be regarded as the founder of ethics.

(*b*) But it was impossible to found scientific ethics without defining at the same time the laws which determine scientific knowledge of every description. Here we reach the essence of the Socratic reform. By returning to reason itself to study the conditions and value of its progress towards truth, that is to say, by the use of logical and critical reflection, Socrates disciplined the philosophic intelligence, showed it the attitude to adopt and the methods to employ in order to attain truth.

The first requisite was to cleanse the mind of the false knowledge which pretends to get to the bottom of things with a few facile ideas. That is why he always began by leading those whom he entangled in the net of his questions to confess their ignorance of that which they had been certain they knew best (Socratic *irony*). But this was merely the preliminary stage of his method. Soon the questioning began afresh, but its object now was to lead Socrates's interlocutor, whose thought it guided in the direction desired, to discover for himself the truth of which he had admitted his ignorance. This was the essence of the Socratic method, his *maieutic*, the art of intellectual midwifery. Moreover, Socrates realised so thoroughly that the attainment of truth is a vital and personal activity, in which the teacher can only assist his pupil's intelligence, as a doctor assists nature, but the latter is the *principal agent*,[1] that he compared the acquisition of knowledge to the awakening of a memory dormant in the soul, a comparison from which Plato was to derive his famous theory of reminiscence (ἀνάμνησις).

How, then, did this maieutic form the philosophic intellect ? By determining its proper object, teaching it to seek the *essences* and definitions of things.[2] Socrates was never weary of recalling reason to this one object : *that which* the subject of discussion is, *what* is courage, piety, virtue, the art of ship-building or cobbling, etc. All these have a being peculiar to themselves, an essence or nature which the human understanding can discover and express by a definition which distinguishes it from everything else. Because Socrates thus required that the essential should in all cases be distinguished from the accidental, and because he persistently employed his intellect in the search for essences, his philosophy may be termed the philosophy of essences. It was no longer a question of reducing everything to water, fire, numbers, or even absolute being, nor yet of finding some indeterminate concept

[1] *Cf.* St. Thomas, *Sum. Theol.*, i, q. 117, a. 1.
[2] *Cf.* Aristotle, *Metaph.*, xi, 4, 1078 b 17–32.

sufficiently elastic to enfold everything like a shapeless mantle. On the contrary, Socrates's aim was to attain the proper intellectual expression of everything—to define and determine its essence by a concept applicable only to itself.

At the same time Socrates taught the reason, if not by a finished theory of ratiocination, or by constructing, as Aristotle would construct later, a logic of syllogism and demonstration, at least practically and of set purpose, to employ concepts, not, as in the barbarous word-play of the sophists, as weapons to deliver strokes at haphazard, but in such a fashion that they fitted exactly the outline and structure of reality. He thus created *dialectic*, an instrument of knowledge, as yet no doubt defective, but which paved the way for the correct notion of scientific knowledge, and was compared by Plato to the art of the expert *chef* who cuts up a fowl by distinguishing and following carefully the smallest joints of its anatomy.

(*c*) Thus this unwearied disputer, for all his superficial scepticism, possessed an invincible confidence in the intellect and in science—but of an intellect disciplined, humble in its attitude towards reality, and a science aware of its limitations, advancing successfully and securely in the apprehension of truth only so far as it respected the sovereignty of the real and was conscious of its ignorance in every direction. In this we recognise Socrates as the teacher of the scientific spirit, as also of the philosophy which we shall learn to know as *moderate intellectualism*. By his logical and critical work he forged the instrument indispensable for the progress of the mind and turned the crisis created by sophistry to the profit and salvation of reason. By his work as a teacher of morality, he not only founded the science of ethics, but liberated thought from the fascination of the sensible, and unintentionally, perhaps, set philosophic speculation on the road to metaphysics, wisdom in the strict sense. This he did simply by raising philosophy (this was the true significance of the Socratic demand for self-knowledge) from exclusive occupation with the physical universe [1] to the study of human nature and human activities, which contain a spiritual element of a higher order altogether than the stars or the entire universe of matter.

But Socrates was no more than a pioneer of genius. He gave the impulse, but never reached the goal. When he died everything was still in the air. For method is not enough, a systematic body of doctrine is necessary ; and Socrates, though his teaching was fertile in fruitful hints, possessed, apart from the elements of ethics, no doctrine in the strict sense. The doctrinal completion of his work and the construction of the true philosophy were reserved for Plato and Aristotle.

[1] Parmenides himself arrived at the metaphysical conception of being by an exclusive consideration of the corporeal universe.

IV

PLATO AND ARISTOTLE

So undoctrinal was Socrates's teaching that his disciples developed it along very divergent lines. The philosophers known as *the minor Socratics*, who seized upon some partial aspect of the Master's thought, which they distorted more or less, were either moralists pure and simple (like the Cyrenaics,[1] who placed man's last end in the pleasure of the moment, and the Cynics,[2] who, going to the opposite extreme, deified force of character or virtue), or logicians infatuated by the love of argument (*eristics*), like the neo-sophists of Elis and especially of the school of Megara,[3] who tended to deny the possibility of knowledge and, by compelling philosophers to find answers to their arguments, indirectly contributed to the progress of logic. The Megarians denied that in any judgment one thing could be predicated of another. According to them, this amounted to affirming that the predicate was the subject and thus everything became identical with

[1] The leading philosophers of this school were Aristippus of Cyrene, Theodore the Atheist, Hegesias, and Anniceris.

[2] The name was derived from the gymnasium in Athens (Κυνόσαργες) where Antisthenes taught. The chief Cynics were Antisthenes (born 445 B.C.), Diogenes of Sinope (400–323), and Crates of Thebes.

[3] The principal representatives of the school of Elis were Phaedo and Menedemus, of the Megarian, Euclid of Megara (not to be confused with Euclid the geometrician), Eubulides of Miletus, Diodorus Cronos, and Stilpo.

74

everything else. Hence *being exists* is the sole legitimate proposition, and the Eleatic metaphysics the only true philosophy.

PLATO

The appellation *major Socratics* belongs only to Plato, Socrates's intellectual heir, and his disciples. *Plato* (427-347),[1] whose father was of royal descent and whose mother traced her pedigree to Solon, ambitious to reign as king in the intellectual domain, endeavoured to combine in the powerful unity of an original system the entire host of speculations which he found scattered and fragmentary in the conflicting systems of his philosophic predecessors. With him philosophy attained her majority. But the work which he attempted and which the Socratic reform had made possible remained incomplete and defective. Under the impulse of his lofty and daring genius, the intellect soared too fast and too high, and failed to achieve by a final victory the conquest of reality.

(a) Like Parmenides, Plato understood that the subject of metaphysics is being itself. But he refused to absorb everything which exists in the unity of immutable and absolute being. And he was thus led to the discovery of important metaphysical truths. He perceived that, since things are more or less perfect, more or less beautiful and good, more or less deserving of love, and since there are things whose goodness is mixed with evil—which in philosophic terminology *participate* in goodness—there must neces-

---

[1] After extensive travels, Plato settled in Athens, where he purchased the estate of a certain Academus to be the home of his school, known therefore as the Academy.

sarily exist a being in which goodness, beauty, and perfection are full and entire, unmingled with their contraries, a being which is the ground of the beauty and goodness of everything else. His thought thus ascended to the true God transcending the world and distinct from it, whom he saw as goodness itself, the *absolute good*, the good, so to speak, in person. But this was not the most prominent aspect of Platonism. As we pointed out above, Socrates's philosophy —a philosophy rather suggested by his practice than formulated theoretically—was the philosophy of essences ; Plato's philosophy was, before everything else, the philosophy of *ideas*.

Socrates had shown that what we must seek and attain at all cost are the essences of things which the mind apprehends and expresses in a definition. What, then, is it which the intellect perceives when it apprehends the essence of a man, a triangle, white, or virtue ? Clearly *man*, abstracting from Peter, Paul, John, etc., *triangle*, abstracting from any particular triangle, isosceles or equilateral, and similarly *white* and *virtue*. Moreover, the concept or idea of *man* or *triangle* persists the same when applied to a host of men or triangles individually different. In other words, these ideas are *universals*. Further, they are immutable and eternal in this sense, that even if, for example, no actual triangle existed, the idea of *triangle*, with all the geometrical truths it involves, would remain eternally the same. Moreover, these ideas enable us to contemplate, pure and unalloyed, the humanity, triangularity, etc., in which the different beings we know as men, triangles, etc., participate. Failing to analyse with sufficient accuracy the nature

intellectual knowledge (νόησις), which is concerned with intelligible things and is itself subdivided into *reason* (διάνοια), whose object is mathematical number, and *intellect* (νοῦς), which rises by means of dialectic to the intuitive contemplation of the idea-essences and finally of God, the super-essential good.

Plato had now to explain this intellectual knowledge, the origin of the ideas in our minds, images of the eternal ideas. Since these ideas cannot be derived from the senses, which are fettered to illusion, we must receive them immediately from on high, and they must be *innate* in our soul. In a former existence, before its union with the body, the soul beheld the ideas and possessed intuitive knowledge. That knowledge still remains with us, but, clouded and darkened by the life of the body, it abides in the soul as a dormant memory, and it is by gradually reviving it that the quest of wisdom enables us to reconquer our original intuition of truth. Thus man is a pure spirit forcibly united with a body, as it were an angel imprisoned in the flesh (*psychological dualism*). The human soul lived before it animated the body, to which it is tied as a punishment for some pre-natal sin, and after death it enters another body; for, while Plato believed in the immortality of the soul, he also held the Pythagorean tenet of transmigration, or metempsychosis.

Since the physical world is not an object of knowledge, Plato can speak of it only in fables or myths, which he develops with all the resources of a consummate art, although they serve only to disguise the impotence of his philosophy to account for material reality.

It is in his myths that he ascribes the production, or rather the organisation, of the world to a *demiurge*— whom, in the opinion of many commentators, he regarded as distinct from God and inferior to him— and expounds the queer notion that man is the origin of all living organisms : the first men created by the gods were of the male sex ; those who led evil lives were changed after death into women, who, in turn, if they continued to sin, were changed into irrational brutes, perhaps even into plants.

In ethics Plato, like his master Socrates, but more clearly than he, established the fundamental truth of moral philosophy : neither pleasure nor virtue nor any partial good, but God himself, and God alone, is the good of man. But how does man attain his good ? By making himself, Plato replied, as like as possible to God by means of virtue and contemplation. Plato also examined, though inadequately, the concept of virtue, and outlined the theory of the four cardinal virtues, prudence, justice, fortitude, and temperance. He taught that it is better to suffer than commit injustice, and in the *Republic* [1] he paints so sublime and so flawless a portrait of the righteous sufferer that it is as though he had caught a glimpse of the Divine Face. But, as a result of his exaggerated intellectualism, he failed to distinguish the acts of the practical from those of the speculative intellect and identified virtue, which requires rectitude of the will, with knowledge, which is a perfection of the reason alone. He there- fore misapplied the principle, in itself true, that the will always follows the guidance of the understanding, and maintained that sin is simply due to lack of know-

ii, 362 A

ledge and that no one deliberately does evil : " the sinner is merely an ignorant person." The consequence of this theory, which Plato did not intend, is the denial of free will.

Plato's sociology betrays the same idealist and rationalist tendency which leads him to misapply another true principle, namely, that the part exists for the whole ; so that in his ideal republic, governed by philosophers, individuals are entirely subordinated to the good of the state, which alone is capable of rights, and disposes despotically of every possible species of property, not only the material possessions, but even the women and children, the life and liberty, of its citizens (*absolute communism*).

(*c*) The radical source of Plato's errors seems to have been his exaggerated devotion to mathematics, which led him to despise empirical reality. They were also due to an over-ambitious view of the scope of philosophy, in which Plato, like the sages of the East, though with greater moderation and discretion, placed the purification, salvation, and life of the entire man.

Moreover, it is on account of these false principles latent in his system that all those philosophic dreams which tend in one way or another to treat man as a pure spirit can be traced directly or indirectly to Plato.

But of Plato himself we may say that his false principles grew in an atmosphere too pure to allow them to yield their full fruit and poison the essence of his thought. St. Augustine was therefore able to extract from Plato's gold-mine the ore of truth.

Plato's thought worked on a large scale and sought to embrace all things in a single grasp. But his superior wisdom and amazing gift of intuition prevented him from fixing in a final and definite statement of doctrine many a speculation which floated vaguely before his mind. Weak points on which another philosopher would have insisted he touched lightly. Hence what in itself is a mark of imperfection—vagueness, imprecision, hints, never worked out, with which he is often satisfied, a method of exposition more aesthetic than scientific, employing only metaphors and symbols, a method which St. Thomas with good reason criticises severely [1]—was actually his safeguard, preserving him from a too disastrous distortion of the truths he had discovered. From this point of view it may be said that Platonism is false, if regarded in *esse* as a fully developed system, but, if regarded in *fieri* as a progress towards a goal beyond itself, of the utmost value as a stage in the development of the true philosophy.

ARISTOTLE

To extract the truth latent in Platonism was the mighty reform effected by *Aristotle*. Aristotle successfully took to pieces Plato's system, adapted to the exigencies of reality the formal principles he had discovered and misapplied, reduced his sweeping perspectives within the limits imposed by a sublime common sense, and thus saved everything vital in his

[1] *Plato habuit malum modum docendi ; omnia enim figurate dicit et per symbola, intendens aliud per verba, quam sonent ipsa verba.* (St. Thomas, *In I De Anima*, viii.)

master's thought. He did more : he founded for all time the true philosophy. If he saved whatever was true and valuable, not only in Plato, but in all the ancient thinkers of Greece, and brought to a successful conclusion the great work of synthesis which Plato had attempted, it was because he definitively secured the attainment of reality by the human intellect. His work was not only the natural fruit of Greek wisdom purified from Plato's mistakes and the alien elements included in Platonism ; it contained, completely formed and potentially capable of unlimited growth, the body of the universal human philosophy.

Before Aristotle, philosophy may be regarded as in an embryonic stage and in process of coming to birth. Thenceforward, its formation complete, it was capable of indefinite development, and knew no bounds. *Inventum philosophicum semper perfectibile.*

In fact, Greek speculation after Aristotle had spent its force, and was unable to keep firm hold of the truth. It would receive considerable material enrichment, but in essentials would deform instead of perfecting philosophy.[1]

(a) For twenty years Aristotle was Plato's disciple ; but he was a disciple with the equipment of a formidable critic. No one has refuted Plato's idealism more powerfully than he, or more effectively demolished a system which places the substance of things outside themselves.

It is perfectly true that the primary object of the intellect is, as Socrates taught, the essences of things ;

[1] This is the reason why we have ended with Aristotle this introductory sketch of the history of philosophy, or more exactly of the formation of philosophy.

perfectly true also, as Plato had perceived, that the essence of Peter, Paul, or John is humanity or human nature, abstracting from the individual characteristics peculiar to Peter, Paul, or John. But this essence as a universal exists only in the intellect—in our mind,[1] which extracts or abstracts it from the things in which it exists individualised [2]—and, on the other hand, it is solely as an object of intelligence (inasmuch as it cannot be conceived apart from certain attributes), and not in its real existence, that it is eternal and necessary. Therefore the essences of perishable things possess no separate existence in the pure state, and the entire Platonic world of archetypal ideas is sheer fiction. The truth of the matter is, as we shall prove later in detail, that there exists in everything an intelligible and immaterial element, which Aristotle calls *form*, in virtue of which it possesses a specific nature or essence. But this principle is not separate from things ; it inheres in them as one of the factors which constitute their substance. Thus individual objects, though mutable and mortal, are no longer deceptive shadows ; they are reality.

If real objects of a higher order exist, none are more immediately accessible to our knowledge. If the sensible world be, as it were, an imperfect likeness of the divine life of pure spirit, it is a being which resembles another being, not a mere image which has no existence in itself. If the world is subject to becoming, it is not pure becoming, but contains

---

[1] And primarily in the Divine Intellect, as the Schoolmen were to explain, thus taking account of the truth contained in Plato's *exemplarism*.

[2] *Cf.* St. Thomas, *In I Metaph.*, l. 10, 158 (ed. Cathala).

enduring and substantial realities. If there is no science of the individual object of sense as such, nevertheless a science of sensible reality is possible, because there exists, incarnate, so to speak, in that reality, something intelligible and immaterial.

Thus the corporeal universe is the object not of mere opinion, which can be expressed only by myth and allegory, but of scientific knowledge, the science of physics. Aristotle was the true founder of physics.[1] His incomparably powerful genius viewed mobility in the immutable light of intellect, showed that all change obeys unchanging laws, laid bare the nature of motion itself, of generation and corruption, and distinguished the four species of causation operative in the sensible world.

In language strangely trenchant and severe, he sums up his long polemic against the doctrine of ideas. Plato, he argues, completely misconceived the nature of the formal cause when he separated it from things. While he fancied " he was stating the substance of perceptible things," he asserted " the existence of a second class of substances," and his " account of the way in which they are the substances of perceptible things is empty talk ; for ' sharing ' (participating) means nothing." He thus made it impossible to give a satisfactory account of nature, and, by attributing all causation and all true reality to the ideas, he was unable to distinguish in the activity of things the respective parts played by the efficient and the final

[1] Aristotle's experimental physics (the science of phenomena) is a magnificent intellectual construction totally ruined by mistakes of fact. But his philosophical physics (the science of moving being as such) lays down the foundations and principles of every true philosophy of nature.

cause. He thus neglected " the efficient cause which is the principle of change." He further failed to give any account of the cause of " that which we see to be the cause in the case of the arts, for the sake of which mind and nature produce all that they do produce." For " mathematics has come to be the whole of philosophy for modern thinkers, and they profess to explain all other things by mathematics." " And as to motion, if the ideas are motionless," there is no archetype of motion in the world of ideas, but in that case " whence," according to the Platonists, " did motion come ? If we cannot explain motion, the whole study of nature has been annihilated." [1]

Refutation of the theory of ideas logically involved the criticism and correction of all the other parts of the Platonic system. In epistemology Aristotle showed that physics, mathematics, and metaphysics, or the first philosophy, are indeed three distinct sciences, but that they are distinguished by their subject-matter, not by the faculty employed, which in all alike is reason. But his most important achievement in this sphere was to prove, by the marvellous analysis of *abstraction* which dominates his entire philosophy, that our ideas are not innate memories of pre-natal experience, but derived from the senses by an activity of the mind.

In psychology, if in his reaction against Plato's *metempsychosis*, and from an excessive caution, he refrained from inquiring into the condition of the soul after death, at least he laid the firm foundations of the spiritualist doctrine by proving, on the one hand, in opposition to Plato's dualism, the substantial unity of

[1] *Metaph.*, i, 9, 992 a 25 – 992 b 10.

the human being, composed of two substantial parts incomplete and complementary, and, on the other, against the materialists, the spiritual nature of the operations of the understanding and will. He thus created the only psychology capable of assimilating and explaining the vast màterial accumulated by modern experiments.

In ethics, by distinguishing between the *speculative judgment* (which proceeds from the understanding alone) and the *practical judgment* (which proceeds conjointly from the will), he showed how free will is possible, and how the sinner does what he knows to be evil, and drew, especially in his treatment of the cardinal virtues and in his analysis of human acts, the outlines of what was to be, so far as the natural order is concerned, the ethics of Christianity.

(*b*) But Aristotle must be studied, not only in his attitude to Plato, but absolutely in his attitude to *that which is*. For Plato did no more than furnish him with the occasion to wrestle with the problem of being. Aristotle won the match, leaving us his great concepts of *potentiality* and *act*, *matter* and *form*, the *categories*, the *transcendentals*, the *causes*, as weapons wherewith to wage the same intellectual contest, and teaching us, as a true master of wisdom, to rise above the study of visible and perishable things to contemplation of the living, imperishable reality which knows no change. " Immovable in its pure activity, this being is in no way subject to change. . . . On such a principle depend the heavens and the world of nature. Its life is such as the best which we enjoy, and enjoy for but a short time. For it is ever in this state, since its act is also pleasure—the act of the supreme intelligence, pure thought thinking itself. . . . If God is always in that good state in which we sometimes are, this compels our wonder ; and if in a better, this is yet more wonderful. Life also belongs to God : for the act of thought is life, and God is that act ; and God's essential act is life most good and eternal. We say therefore that God is a living being, eternal and perfect, so that life which endures everlastingly belongs to God, for God is this life." [1] Moreover, this God is perfectly one, absolutely single. " Those who say mathematical number is first, and go on to generate one kind of substance after another and give different principles for each, make the substance of the universe a mere series of episodes and they give us many governing principles ; but the world must not be governed badly. As Homer observed, *the rule of many is not good ; one is the ruler.*" [2]

Thus Aristotle, as Alexander of Aphrodisias remarks in a fine passage of his *Commentary on the Metaphysics*,[3] " leads us from the things which are themselves on the lowest plane, but most familiar to us, up to the Father, who has made all things, to God the most sublime, and proves that as the founder is the cause of the unity of the globe and the brass, so the Divine Power, author of unity and maker of all things, is for all beings the cause of their being what they are."

Aristotle's mind was at once extremely practical and extremely metaphysical. A rigorous logician, but also a keen-sighted realist, he gladly respected the

---

[1] *Metaph.*, xii, 7, 1072 b ; 9, 1074 b 35.
[2] *Metaph.*, xii, 10, 1076 a.
[3] Alexander of Aphrodisias, *In Metaph.*, ad 1045 a 36.

demands of the actual, and found room in his speculation for every variety of being without violating or distorting the facts at any point, displaying an intellectual vigour and freedom to be surpassed only by the crystalline lucidity and angelic force of St. Thomas Aquinas. But this vast wealth is arranged in the light of principles, mastered, classified, measured, and dominated by the intellect. It is the masterpiece of wisdom, a wisdom which is still wholly human, but nevertheless, from its lofty throne, embraces with a single glance the totality of things.

Aristotle, however, was a profound rather than a comprehensive thinker. He took little care to display the proportions and wide perspectives of his philosophy; his primary object was to apprehend by an absolutely reliable method and with a faultless precision what in every nature accessible to human knowledge is most characteristic, most intimate—in short, most truly itself. Therefore he not only organised human knowledge, and laid the solid foundations of logic, biology, psychology, natural history, metaphysics, ethics, and politics, but also cut and polished a host of precious definitions and conclusions sparkling with the fires of reality.

It can therefore be affirmed without hesitation that among philosophers Aristotle holds a position altogether apart : genius, gifts, and achievement—all are unique. It is the law of nature that the sublime is difficult to achieve and that what is difficult is rare. But when a task is of extraordinary difficulty both in itself and in the conditions it requires, we may expect that there will be but one workman capable of its accomplishment. Moreover, a well-built edifice is usually built not on the plans of several architects, but on the plan of a single one. If, therefore, the edifice of human wisdom or philosophy is to be adequately constructed, the foundations must be laid once for all by a single thinker. On these foundations thousands of builders will be able to build in turn, for the growth of knowledge represents the labour of generations and will never be complete. But there can be but one master-builder.[1]

For that reason, in spite of the mistakes, defects, and gaps which betray in his work the limitations of human reason,[2] Aristotle is as truly the

[1] Descartes remarks very truly in his *Discours de la Méthode* : " Works composed of many pieces and made by the hand of several workmen are not so perfect as those which are the work of a single individual."

But he was wrong in believing (i) that he was the man destined to lay the foundation of philosophy, a work which the ancients had failed to accomplish ; (ii) that by himself he was competent—at least, given sufficient time and experience—not only to lay the foundation of science, but to complete the edifice ; and (iii) in rejecting contemptuously the entire achievement of preceding generations, together with the traditional wisdom of humanity. Aristotle, on the contrary, succeeded in his task by constant criticism and analysis of his predecessors' thought, and by making use of the accumulated results of human speculation in the past.

[2] Aristotle is often credited with certain errors made by his disciples or commentators, especially about the human soul and the divine knowledge and causality. But a careful study of the text proves that when the philosopher maintained that the intellect is separate, he meant that it is separate from matter, not from the soul itself (*cf.* St. Thomas, *In III De Anima*, 4 and 5), and therefore he did not deny, as is often asserted, the personal immortality of the human soul (*cf.* also *Metaph.*, xii, 3, 1070 a 26). Nor did he teach that God is not the efficient cause of the world and moves it only as the end, or good, which it desires. (The passage in the *Metaph.*, xii, 7, means simply that God moves as final cause or object of love the intelligence which moves the first heaven ; he does not affirm that God can act only as final cause and has not made things. On the contrary, in *Metaph.*, ii, 1, 993 b 28, he says that the heavenly bodies are dependent on the first cause, not only

philosopher *par excellence,* as St. Thomas is the theologian.[1]

for their motion, but for their very being. *Cf. Metaph.* vi, 1, 1026 b 17.)
Cf. also the passage from Alexander of Aphrodisias, quoted above in the text, in which God's efficient causality in Aristotle's system is admirably brought out. As for the passage (*Metaph.,* xii, 9) in which Aristotle investigates the formal object of the Divine Intellect, remarking that it is better not to know than to know certain things of a lower order, it most certainly does not amount to the denial that God knows the things of the world ; the statement is put forward simply to prepare for the solution of the question discussed. That solution, as indicated by Aristotle, is formally true, and consists in the proposition, which St. Thomas later affirmed more explicitly, that the Divine Intellect, because of its absolute independence, has no other formal object than the Divine Essence itself, and therefore does not know the things of the world in themselves, but in that essence in which everything is life.

It remains true, nevertheless, that Aristotle committed serious errors (for instance, his attempt to prove the existence of the world *ab aeterno*), and was also guilty of many omissions. In particular, the doctrine of creation, which follows with absolute necessity from his principles, is nowhere explicitly formulated by him (indeed, no heathen philosopher reached a clear notion of creation *ex nihilo*); and on those questions which, though in themselves capable of rational proof, are most difficult to solve without the aid of revelation—the relation of the world to God, the lot of the soul after death—he maintained a reserve, which was perhaps very prudent in itself, but leaves his work manifestly incomplete.

[1] Goethe, repeating the theme of Raphael's wonderful *School of Athens,* in which Plato is depicted as an inspired old man, his face turned heavenward, Aristotle as a man in the full vigour of youth pointing triumphantly to the earth and its realities, has drawn in his *Theory of Colours* (Part 2, *Ueberliefertes*) a striking comparison between Plato and Aristotle. " Plato," he says, " seems to behave as a spirit descended from heaven, who has chosen to dwell a space on earth. He hardly attempts to know this world. He has already formed an idea of it, and his chief desire is to communicate to mankind, which stands in such need of them, the truths which he has brought with him and delights to impart. If he penetrates to the depth of things, it is to fill them with his own soul, not to analyse them. Without intermission and with the burning ardour of his spirit, he aspires to rise and regain the heavenly abode from which he came down. The aim of all his

(*c*) Aristotle was born in 384 at Stagira, in Thrace. The son of a doctor, by name Nicomachus, he belonged to the family of the Asclepiadae, descended, it was said, from Aesculapius. At the age of eighteen he became a pupil of Plato, whose lectures he attended until his death (347). After Plato's death he went to live at Atarneus in Mysia where Hermias was king, and from there to Mytilene. He then spent eight years at the court of King Philip of Macedon, where he became Alexander's tutor. After his pupil's accession to the throne, he settled in Athens, where he established his school at the Lyceum (a gymnasium consecrated to Apollo Lycaeus). He taught as he walked to and fro with his pupils under the trees of the Lyceum, whence the name *Peripatetics* (walkers) by which his disciples became known. He spent twelve years in Athens. When the party opposed

discourse is to awaken in his hearers the notion of a single eternal being, of the good, of truth, of beauty. His method and words seem to melt, to dissolve into vapour, whatever scientific facts he has managed to borrow from the earth.

" Aristotle's attitude towards the world is, on the other hand, entirely human. He behaves like an architect in charge of a building. Since he is on earth, on earth he must work and build. He makes certain of the nature of the ground, but only to the depth of his foundations. Whatever lies beyond to the centre of the earth does not concern him. He gives his edifice an ample foundation, seeks his materials in every direction, sorts them, and builds gradually. He therefore rises like a regular pyramid, whereas Plato ascends rapidly heavenward like an obelisk or a sharp tongue of flame.

"Thus have these two men, representing qualities equally precious and rarely found together, divided mankind, so to speak, between them."

[1] " We must remember, moreover, that Stagira, a city of Chalcidice, was a Greek colony where Greek was spoken. It is therefore incorrect to regard Aristotle, as he is sometimes regarded, as only half Greek. He was a pure Hellene, as pure as Parmenides, for example, or Anaxagoras." (Hamelin, *Le Système d'Aristote*, p. 4.)

to the Macedonians brought against him an accusation of impiety, on the pretext of a hymn he had once composed on the death of his friend Hermias, he retired to Chalcis, where he died at the age of sixty-three (322).

The story is told of him that his love of study was so great that he devised the plan of holding in his hand, while at work, a ball of copper which, if he fell asleep, would rouse him by falling into a metal basin. To assist his researches Philip and Alexander placed their vast resources at his disposal. He wrote books to be read by the general public (*dialogues*), which are all lost—Cicero praised their style in the highest terms : *flumen aureum orationis fundens Aristoteles* (*Acad.*, II, 38, 119)—and *acroamatic* books, in which he summarised the lectures given to his disciples ; the majority of these have survived.[1]

The history of these books, as related by Strabo, is very strange, and illustrates, as aptly as Pascal's remark on Cleopatra's nose, the part played by trifling

[1] The following is a list of Aristotle's works :—

i. The collection of works dealing with Logic and known collectively by the name of *Organon* (instrument of scientific knowledge). They consist of the Κατηγορίαι, the *Categories* ; the Ἀναλύτικα πρότερα καὶ ὕστερα, the *Prior and Posterior Analytics* ; the Τόπικα, the *Topics* ; the Περὶ σοφιστικῶν ἐλέγχων, *On Sophistic Arguments* ; and the Περὶ ἑρμηνείας, *On Interpretation, De Interpretatione*, a treatise on the meaning of propositions, which in spite of Andronicus's rejection must be accepted as authentic.

ii. The *Physics*, Φυσικὴ ἀκρόασις (the authenticity of Book 7 is doubtful), with which we must group the following treatises : *On the Heavens* (*De Caelo*), Περὶ οὐρανοῦ ; *On Generation and Corruption*, Περὶ γενεσέως καὶ φθορᾶς ; *On the Parts of Animals*, Περὶ ζῴων μόριων ; *On the Soul*, Περὶ ψυχῆς ; *On Sensation*, Περὶ αἰσθήσεως καὶ αἰσθητῶν ; *On Memory*, Περὶ μνήμης καὶ ἀναμνήσεως ; the *Meteorology*, Μετεωρολογικά ; the *History of Animals*, Περὶ τὰ ζῷα ἰστορίαι (the authenticity of Book 10 is doubtful) ; and many other treatises, several of which are of dubious

accidents in determining the destinies of mankind. At the philosopher's death they were inherited together with his library by his disciple and successor Theophrastus. Theophrastus bequeathed them to a disciple

authenticity, especially the *De Mundo*. (The treatise on *Physiognomy* is spurious, but is apparently a compilation from authentic fragments.)

iii. The *Metaphysics*, Τὰ μετὰ τὰ φυσικά, of which the second book, α ἔλαττον, is the work of a disciple, Pasicles of Rhodes.

iv. The *Nicomachean Ethics*, Ἠθικὰ Νικομάχεια, and the *Eudemian Ethics*, Ἠθικὰ Εὐδήμεια. The latter work was composed, not by Aristotle, but by Eudemus himself. To these we may add the *Great Ethics* (*Magna Moralia*), Ἠθικὰ μεγάλα, which is a *résumé* of the two preceding, and therefore not written by Aristotle ; the *Politics*, Πολιτικά ; the *Poetics*, Περὶ ποιητικῆς ; and the *Rhetoric*, Τέχνη ῥητορική. The treatise *On Virtues and Vices*, the *Economics*, and the *Rhetoric to Alexander* are spurious. In 1891 was discovered and published the *Constitution of Athens*, Ἀθηναίων πολιτεία. It formed part of a collection in which Aristotle gave an outline of the constitutions of 158 Greek states.

Of the Schoolmen who commented on the works of Aristotle, the most important are Albertus Magnus, St. Thomas, and Silvester Maurus, whose paraphrase and commentary following the text word for word may still be usefully consulted. Saint Thomas wrote commentaries : (*a*) on the *De Interpretatione* (unfinished and replaced by Cajetan's for lessons 3–14 of Book 2) ; (*b*) on the *Posterior Analytics* ; (*c*) on the *Physics* ; (*d*) on the *De Caelo et Mundo* (St. Thomas died before it was completed, and from Book 3, lesson 8, the commentary was continued by his pupil, Peter of Auvergne) ; (*e*) on the *Generation and Corruption of Animals* (St. Thomas's unfinished *Commentary* has been completed by passages borrowed from other writers, in particular from the *Commentary* of Albertus Magnus) ; (*f*) on the *Meteorology* (completed by another hand from Bk. 2, lesson 11); (*g*) on the *De Anima* (the commentary on Books 2 and 3 is by St. Thomas himself, the commentary on Bk. 1 compiled from his lectures by one of his pupils, Raynald of Piperno ; (*h*) on the *Parva Naturalia* (*De Sensu et Sensato, de Memoria et Reminiscentia, de Somno et Vigilia*) ; (*i*) on the *Metaphysics* (modern edition by Padre Cathala, Turin, Marietti, 1915) ; (*j*) on the *Nicomachean Ethics* ; (*k*) on the *Politics* (completed by Peter of Auvergne from Bk. 3, lesson 6, or, as others think from Bk. 4). *Cf.* De Rubeis, *Dissert. 23* in vol. i, *Op. Omn. S. Thomae Aq.*, Leonine edition.

For the writings of St. Thomas and the authenticity of his various minor works, see Mandonnet, O.P., *Des Écrits authentiques de Saint Thomas* (reprinted from the *Revue Thomiste*, 1909–1910) Friburg.

named Neleus, Neleus in turn to his heirs. The latter, fearing they might be seized for the royal library at Pergamum, hid them in an underground chamber. They died and the manuscripts were lost. They remained lost for a century and a half and were only recovered by the good fortune of a successful book-lover. About the year 100 B.C. the descendants of Neleus's heirs discovered the manuscripts (in a very bad condition, as we can well imagine) and sold them for a large sum to a wealthy collector, Apellicon of Teos, who published them, in a very faulty edition. At the capture of Athens by the Romans in 86 B.C. they came into the possession of Sulla. The grammarian Tyrannio had access to them and made use of them, and finally Andronicus of Rhodes catalogued and republished them.[1] *Commentaries* were composed by Alexander of Aphrodisias (second century A.D.), also by several neo-Platonic philosophers, Porphyry (third century), Themistius (fourth century), Simplicius, and Philo (sixth century).

[1] Strabo, *Geog.*, xiii, 1, 54 ; Plut. *Sulla*, 26. Strabo's testimony is o considerable weight. It has, however, been proved that some of the most important scientific treatises of Aristotle were known to the Peripatetics and their opponents in the third and second centuries B.C. We must therefore conclude that Strabo's account is reliable in its positive assertions, so far as the history of Aristotle's " acroamatic " manuscripts are concerned, but inaccurate, or at least exaggerated, in its negative statements. More or less complete copies of the Philosopher's works must have been in circulation in the Peripatetic school before Apellicon's discovery. We may nevertheless agree with Hamelin's conclusion that " the scientific writings of Aristotle were little read even by the Peripatetic school in its degeneracy. Apellicon's discovery would have had the effect of making these works once more fashionable." The truth of the matter therefore would be that, before this discovery and the works of Andronicus, Aristotle's scientific treatises were not indeed unknown, as Strabo says, but at any rate little and badly known.

The Scholastic tradition, which grew up from the eighth century onward in the Christian West, was for long ignorant of Aristotle's original works, with the exception of the *Organon* (the treatises on logic), which had been translated into Latin [1] by Boethius (480–526). But it was acquainted with his thought, which had been transmitted and popularised at second hand and formed an integral part of the great philosophic synthesis of late antiquity, Platonic though it was in the main, on which the Fathers, especially St. Augustine, had drawn so largely in the service of the faith. In the Christian schools Aristotle's logic was taught in Boethius's translation. But it was not until the latter part of the twelfth century that the other writings of the Philosopher (*physics, metaphysics, ethics*) began to reach the Schoolmen, mainly, it would appear, as a result of the ardent polemic conducted at that date by the leaders of Christian thought against the philosophy of the Arabs, who possessed these books together with the neo-Platonic commentaries in a Syrian version translated later into Arabic, and appealed to their authority. At first the object of considerable suspicion [2] on account of the source

---

[1] Later Boethius's work was partially lost, and it was not until after 1141 that certain books of the *Organon*, reintroduced from the Arabs, began to appear in the philosophic literature of the Middle Ages, where they formed what was then known as the *Logica Nova*. These were the *Prior and Posterior Analytics*, the *Topics*, and the *Sophistic Arguments*. Cf. de Wulf, *Hist. de la Phil. médiévale*, 2nd ed. pp. 149 sqq.

[2] Censures (issued in 1210 by a council of the province of Sens which met at Paris, and renewed in 1215, in the statute imposed on the University of Paris by the legate Robert de Courçon, a statute confirmed by Gregory IX in 1231 and by Urban IV in 1263) forbade the employment of Aristotle's writings in public lectures or private teaching. We must remember, however, that, as M. Forget points out (*Rapp. au*

from which they had been received and the mistakes which the Arab commentators had foisted into them, all the works of Aristotle were soon translated into Latin, at first from the Arabic text, later [1] from the original Greek.[2]

Now took place the meeting of human wisdom and divine truth, of Aristotle and the Faith. All truth belongs of right to Christian thought, as the spoils of the Egyptians to the Hebrews. *Quaecunque igitur apud omnes praeclara dicta sunt, nostra Christianorum sunt,*[3] because according to that saying of St. Ambrose, which St. Thomas delighted to quote, *every truth, whoever said it, comes from the Holy Spirit.*[4] But someone must actually take possession, someone must enrol in

congr. scientif. intern. des cath., Brussels, 1894), individuals remained free to read, study, and comment on these books in private. Moreover, the censures bound only the University of Paris. In 1229 the University of Toulouse, founded and organised under the protection of the papal legate himself, attracted students by announcing lectures on the books forbidden at Paris. Finally, even at Paris, when the faculty of arts included in its course from 1255 public lectures on the *Physics* and *Metaphysics*, ecclesiastical authority made no attempt to interfere. And, more significantly still, Pope Urban IV, a few years later, took under his personal patronage William of Moerbeke's translation of Aristotle and St. Thomas Aquinas's *Commentaries*. See Chollet, " Aristotélisme de la Scolastique " in Vacant and Mangenot's *Dictionnaire de Théologie*, and de Wulf, *op. cit.*, p. 242.

[1] Some of Aristotle's works were apparently read at first in a Latin translation from Arabic, others in a direct translation from the Greek. In any case it was not long before the latter entirely superseded the former. St. Thomas used only direct versions from the Greek.

[2] The best of these translations is that of the entire works of Aristotle made between 1260 and 1270 by William of Moerbeke at the suggestion and under the supervision of St. Thomas. It is an absolutely literal rendering of the Greek text.

[3] St. Justin, *Apol.*, ii, 13.

[4] *Omne verum a quocumque dicatur, a Spiritu sancto est.*

the royal service of Christ the marvellous intellect of Aristotle. This work, begun by Albert the Great (1193–1280), was continued and brought to a successful conclusion by *St. Thomas Aquinas* (1225–1274). Its accomplishment demanded a rare conjunction of favourable conditions—the ripe culture of the age of St. Louis, the magnificent organisation of the Dominican order, the genius of St. Thomas.[1] St. Thomas, whom the Church has proclaimed Doctor *par excellence*, *Doctor Communis Ecclesiae*, and whom she has enthroned as the universal teacher of her schools, was not content with transferring the entire philosophy of Aristotle to the domain of Christian thought, and making it the instrument of a unique theological synthesis ; he raised it in the process to a far higher order, and, so to speak, transfigured it.

He purged it from every trace of error—that is to say, in the philosophic order, for so far as the sciences of observation or phenomena are concerned, St. Thomas was no more able than Aristotle to escape the errors prevalent in his day, errors which do not in any way affect his philosophy itself. He welded it into a powerful and harmonious system ; he explored

---

[1] For the successful performance of such a task it was also requisite that Christian thought should have attained the high degree of elaboration alike in the philosophical and theological order which it had received from the Fathers and the Scholastic predecessors of St. Thomas. Therefore the work of Albertus Magnus and St. Thomas was not to change, but on the contrary to complete Christian philosophy, giving it its mature expression. If contemporaries were primarily impressed with the novelty of their work—a novelty of completion, not of alteration —the reason is that the final process which perfects a system must always come as a shock to those who witness it, and who most likely are attached by force of habit to certain aspects of its imperfect state as such.

its principles, cleared its conclusions, enlarged its horizon ; and, if he rejected nothing, he added much, enriching it with the immense wealth of the Latin Christian tradition, restoring in their proper places many of Plato's doctrines, on certain fundamental points (for example, on the question of essence and existence) opening up entirely new perspectives, and thus giving proof of a philosophic genius as mighty as that of Aristotle himself. Finally, and this was his supreme achievement, when by his genius as a theologian he made use of Aristotle's philosophy as the instrument of the sacred science which is, so to speak, " an impress on our minds of God's own knowledge," [1] he raised that philosophy above itself by submitting it to the illumination of a higher light, which invested its truth with a radiance more divine than human. Between Aristotle as viewed in himself and Aristotle viewed in the writings of St. Thomas is the difference which exists between a city seen by the flare of a torchlight procession and the same city bathed in the light of the morning sun.

For this reason, though St. Thomas is first and foremost a theologian, we may as appropriately, if not with greater propriety, call his philosophy Thomist rather than Aristotelian.

This philosophy of Aristotle and St. Thomas is in fact what a modern philosopher has termed *the natural philosophy of the human mind,* for it develops and brings to perfection what is most deeply and genuinely natural in our intellect alike in its elementary apprehensions and in its native tendency towards truth.

Sum. Theol., i, q. 1, a 3, *ad* 2.

It is also the *evidential* philosophy, based on the double evidence of the data perceived by our senses and our intellectual apprehension of first principles— the philosophy of *being*, entirely supported by and modelled upon what is, and scrupulously respecting every demand of reality—the philosophy of the *intellect*, which it trusts as the faculty which attains truth, and forms by a discipline which is an incomparable mental purification. And for this very reason it proves itself the *universal* philosophy in the sense that it does not reflect a nationality, class, group, temperament, or race, the ambition or melancholy of an individual or any practical need, but is the expression and product of reason, which is everywhere the same ; and in this sense also, that it is capable of leading the finest intellects to the most sublime knowledge and the most difficult of attainment, yet without once betraying those vital convictions, instinctively acquired by every sane mind, which compose the domain, wide as humanity, of common sense. It can therefore claim to be abiding and permanent (*philosophia perennis*) in the sense that before Aristotle and St. Thomas had given it scientific formulation as a systematic philosophy, it existed from the dawn of humanity in germ and in the pre-philosophic state, as an instinct of the understanding and a natural knowledge of the first principles of reason and ever since its foundation as a system has remained firm and progressive, a powerful and living tradition, while all other philosophies have been born and have died in turn. And, finally, it stands out as being, beyond comparison with any other, one ; one because it alone bestows harmony and unity on human knowledge—both metaphysical and scientific—and one because in itself it realises a maximum of consistency in a maximum of complexity, and neglect of the least of its principles involves the most unexpected consequences, distorting our understanding of reality in innumerable directions.

These are a few of the external signs which witness to its truth, even before we have studied it for ourselves and discovered by personal proof its intrinsic certitude and rational necessity.

V

DEFINITION OF PHILOSOPHY

We began by calling philosophy *human wisdom*. Now that the history of its origins has given us further information as to the nature and object of this wisdom, we are in a position to attempt a more precise definition of philosophy.

For this purpose we shall take philosophy to mean philosophy *par excellence*, the first philosophy or *metaphysics*. What we shall say of it in the absolute sense (*simpliciter*) will be applicable relatively (*secundum quid*) to the other departments of philosophy.

Philosophy is not a "wisdom" of conduct or practical life that consists in acting well. It is a wisdom whose nature consists essentially in *knowing*.

How? Knowing in the fullest and strictest sense of the term, that is to say, *with certainty*, and in being able to state why a thing is what it is and cannot be otherwise, knowing *by causes*. The search for causes is indeed the chief business of philosophers, and the knowledge with which they are concerned is not a merely probable knowledge, such as orators impart by their speeches, but a knowledge which compels the assent of the intellect, like the knowledge which the geometrician conveys by his demonstrations. But certain knowledge of causes is termed *science*. Philosophy therefore is a science.

Knowing by what medium, by what light? Knowing by reason, by what is called the *natural light* of the human intellect. This is a quality common to every purely human science (as contrasted with theology). That is to say, the rule of philosophy, its criterion of truth, is the evidence of its object.

The medium or light by which a science knows its objects is termed in technical language its *lumen sub quo*, the light in which it apprehends the object of its knowledge (itself termed the *object, quod*). Each of the different sciences has its own distinctive light (*lumen sub quo, medium seu motivum formale*) which corresponds with the formal principles by means of which they attain their object. But these different principles are alike in this, that they are all known by the spontaneous activity of our intellect, as the natural faculty of knowledge, in other words by the natural light of reason—and not, like the principles of theology, by a supernatural communication made to man (*revelation*), and by the light of faith. We have now to consider the object *quod* of philosophy.

Knowing what ? To answer this question we may recall the subjects which engaged the attention of the different philosophers whose teachings we have summarised. They inquired into everything—knowledge itself and its methods, being and non-being, good and evil, motion, the world, beings animate and inanimate, man and God. Philosophy therefore is concerned with everything, is a *universal* science.

This does not, however, mean that philosophy absorbs all the other sciences, or is the sole science, of which all the rest are merely departments ; nor on the other hand that it is itself absorbed by the other sciences, being no more than their systematic arrangement. On the contrary, philosophy possesses its distinctive nature and object, in virtue of which it differs from the other sciences. If this were not the case philosophy would be a chimera, and those philosophers whose tenets we have briefly sketched would have treated of unreal problems.[1] But that philosophy is something real, and that its problems have the most urgent claim to be studied, is proved by the fact that the human mind is compelled by its very constitution to ask the questions which the philosophers discuss, questions which moreover involve the principles on which the certainty of the conclusions reached by every science in the last resort depends.

" You say," wrote Aristotle in a celebrated dilemma, " one must philosophise. Then you must philosophise. You say one should not philosophise. Then (to prove your contention) you must philosophise. In any case you must philosophise." [2]

---

[1] No doubt they also studied many questions relating to the special sciences, for the differentiation of the sciences had not been carried so far as in modern times. Nevertheless the primary object of their study lay elsewhere, and, at least after Socrates, those special sciences— astronomy, geometry, arithmetic, music, medicine, and geography— which the ancients cultivated with success developed separately, and in clear distinction from philosophy. The very history of the special sciences, which in modern times have made such enormous progress independently of philosophy and as autonomous branches of study, plainly proves that they are no part of the former.

[2] " εἰ μὲν φιλοσοφητέον, φιλοσοφητέον, καὶ, εἰ μὴ φιλοσοφητέον, φιλοσοφητέον, πάντως ἄρα φιλοσοφητέον."

This dilemma is taken from the Προτρεπτικός, a lost work of which only a few fragments have come down to us. (Cf. fr. 50, 1483 b 29, 42; 1484 a 2, 8, 18.)

But how can philosophy be a *special* science if it deals with everything? We must now inquire under what aspect it is concerned with everything, or, to put it another way, what is that which in everything directly and for itself interests the philosopher. If, for example, philosophy studies man, its object is not to ascertain the number of his vertebræ or the causes of his diseases ; that is the business of anatomy and medicine. Philosophy studies man to answer such questions as whether he possesses an intellect which sets him absolutely apart from the other animals, whether he possesses a soul, if he has been made to enjoy God or creatures, etc. When these questions are answered, thought can soar no higher. No problems lie beyond or above these. We may say then that the philosopher does not seek the explanation nearest to the phenomena perceived by our senses, but the explanation most remote from them, the ultimate explanation. This is expressed in philosophical terminology by saying that philosophy is not concerned with *secondary causes* or proximate explanations ; [1] but on the contrary with *first causes*, highest principles or ultimate explanations.

Moreover, when we remember our conclusion that philosophy knows things by the natural light of reason, it is clear that it investigates the first causes or highest principles *in the natural order*.

When we said that philosophy is concerned with everything, everything which exists, every possible object of knowledge, our statement was too indefinite. We determined only the matter with which philosophy

[1] That is to say, approximating to the particulars of sensible phenomena.

deals, its *material* object, but said nothing of the aspect under which it views that object, or the attributes of that object which it studies ; that is to say, we did not define its *formal* object, its formal standpoint. The formal object of a science is the aspect under which it apprehends its object, or, we may say, that which it studies primarily and *intrinsically* and in reference to which it studies everything else ; [1] that which philosophy studies in this formal sense in things, and the standpoint from which it studies everything else, is the *first causes* or highest principles of things in so far as these causes or principles belong to the natural order.

The *material object* of a faculty, science, art, or virtue, is simply the thing or subject-matter—without further qualification—with which that faculty, science, art, or virtue, deals. For instance, the material object of chemistry is *inorganic bodies* ; of the faculty of sight, *objects within our range of vision*. But this does not enable us to distinguish between chemistry and physics, which is also concerned with inorganic bodies, or between sight and touch. To obtain an exact definition of chemistry we must define its object as the intrinsic or substantial changes of inorganic bodies, and similarly the object of sight as colour. We have now defined the *formal object* (*objectum formale quod*), that is to say, that which immediately and of its very nature, or intrinsically and directly, or again necessarily and primarily (these expressions are equivalent renderings of the Latin formula *per se primo*), is apprehended or studied in things by a particular science,

---

[1] *Quod per se primo haec scientia considerat et sub cujus ratione caetera omnia cognoscit.*

art, or faculty, and in reference to which it apprehends or studies everything else.

Thus philosophy, alone among the branches of human knowledge, has for its object everything which is. But in everything which is it investigates only the first causes. The other sciences, on the contrary, have for their object some particular province of being, of which they investigate only the secondary causes or proximate principles. That is to say, of all branches of human knowledge philosophy is the most sublime.

It follows further that philosophy is in strictest truth *wisdom*, for it is the province of wisdom to study the highest causes : *sapientis est altissimas causas considerare.* It thus grasps the entire universe in a small number of principles and enriches the intellect without burdening it.

The account we have just given is applicable in an unqualified sense only to the first philosophy or metaphysics, but may be extended to philosophy in general, if it is regarded as a body of which metaphysics is the head.[1] We shall then define philosophy in general as a universal body of sciences [2] whose formal stand-

[1] The ancients understood by the term *philosophy* the sum-total of the main branches of scientific study (*physics*, or the science of nature ; *mathematics*, or the sciences of proportion ; *metaphysics*, or the science of being as such ; *logic* ; and *ethics*). There could therefore be no question of distinguishing between philosophy and the sciences. The one question with which they were concerned was how to distinguish the first philosophy, or metaphysics, from the other sciences. We, on the contrary, since the enormous development of the special sciences, must distinguish from them not only metaphysics (the science of absolutely first principles) but the study of the first principles in a particular order (for instance, the mathematical or the physical) ; and the entire body of these constitutes what we call philosophy.

[2] Only metaphysics and logic constitute a universal science specifically one.

point[1] is first causes (whether absolutely first causes or principles, the formal object of metaphysics, or the first causes in a particular order, the formal object of the other branches of philosophy). And it follows that metaphysics alone deserves the name of *wisdom* absolutely speaking (*simpliciter*), the remaining branches of philosophy only relatively or from a particular point of view (*secundum quid*).

> *Conclusion I.*—Philosophy is the science which by the natural light of reason studies the first causes or highest principles of all things—is, in other words, the science of things in their first causes, in so far as these belong to the natural order.

The difficulty of such a science is proportionate to its elevation. That is why the philosopher, just because the object of his studies is the most sublime, should personally be the humblest of students, a humility, however, which should not prevent his defending, as it is his duty to do, the sovereign dignity of wisdom as the queen of sciences.

The perception that the sphere of philosophy is

[1] Strictly speaking, there is no one formal object of philosophy, since philosophy as a whole is not simply one, but a compound of several distinct sciences (*logic, natural philosophy, metaphysics*, etc.), each specified by a distinct formal object (*ens rationis logicum, ens mobile, ens in quantum ens—cf.* Part II). But between the formal objects of the different philosophic sciences there is something analogously common— the fact that they study, each in its own order, the highest and most universal causes, and treat their subject-matter from the standpoint of these causes. We may therefore say that the highest causes constitute the final object or the formal standpoint analogously common of philosophy taken as a whole.

universal led Descartes (seventeenth century) to regard philosophy as the sole science[1] of which the others were but parts ; Auguste Comte, on the contrary, and the positivists generally (nineteenth century), sought to absorb it in the other sciences, as being merely their " systematisation." It is evident that the cause of both errors was the failure to distinguish between the material and formal object of philosophy.

Philosophy of Aristotle and St. Thomas

Philosophy and the *corpus* of other sciences have the same material object (everything knowable). But the formal object of philosophy is first causes, of the other sciences secondary causes.

Descartes	*Auguste Comte*
Philosophy absorbs the other sciences—is the whole of science.	The sciences absorb philosophy—there is no philosophy.

We said above that philosophy is a science, and that it attains certain knowledge. By this we would not be understood to claim that philosophy provides certain solutions for *every* question that can be asked within its domain. On many points the philosopher

---

[1] Descartes used the term " philosophy " in its ancient sense. For the ancients, as for Descartes, the word denoted the entire body of scientific knowledge. But the ancients divided philosophy thus understood into several distinct sciences, among which metaphysics was distinguished as in the fullest sense philosophy. Descartes, on the contrary, regarded philosophy, still understood as the entire body of scientific knowledge, as a science specifically one (of which metaphysics, physics, mechanics, medicine, and ethics were the principal subdivisions). He thus recognised only one science. In our view philosophy is a body of sciences which owes its unity and distinction from the other sciences to its formal standpoint (first causes). The leading member of this body of sciences is metaphysics, a science specifically one, whose formal object is universal (being *qua* being).

must be content with probable solutions, either because the question goes beyond the actual scope of his science, for example in many sections of natural philosophy and psychology, or because of its nature it admits only of a probable answer, for example the application of moral rules to individual cases. But this element of mere probability is accidental to science as such. And philosophy yields a greater number of certain conclusions, and of those many more perfect, namely, the conclusions of metaphysics, than any other purely human science.

VI

PHILOSOPHY AND THE SPECIAL SCIENCES

WE have now to define the relationship between philosophy (particularly the first philosophy or metaphysics) and the other sciences.

Every science is mistress in her own house, inasmuch as every science possesses the indispensable and sufficient means of attaining truth within its own sphere and no one is entitled to deny the truths thus proved.

A science, however, or rather a scientist, may happen to make a mistake in its own domain. In such a case the science in question is no doubt competent to judge and correct itself, but it is obvious that a superior science has also the right to judge and correct it, if the mistake should contradict one of its own results and thus come under its jurisdiction. But philosophy, and especially philosophy in the highest sense, that is metaphysics, is the sovereign science. Therefore it is competent to judge every other human science, rejecting as false every scientific hypothesis which contradicts its own results.

Take for example an hypothesis of physics which appears to contradict a truth of philosophy.[1] Physics is competent to judge that hypothesis by the laws of

[1] It may, for instance, be questioned whether the law of *inertia*, as formulated since Galileo and Descartes, can be reconciled with the axiom of philosophy : *quidquid movetur ab alio movetur*.

physics, but philosophy is also competent to judge it by the principles of philosophy, determining whether and how far it really contradicts the philosophic truth in question. (If the contradiction is real, it is evident that the hypothesis of physics in question must be false, for one truth cannot contradict another. The physicist must therefore bow to the verdict of philosophy, revise his arguments and make further experiments.[1])

Let us now take a conclusion of philosophy which appears to contradict a truth established by physics.[2] It is for philosophy to judge that conclusion in accordance with the principles of philosophy, to decide whether and how far it is really in conflict with the physical truth in question. But physics is incompetent to determine the question by the principles and data of physics. (If the contradiction is real, it is obvious that the alleged conclusion of philosophy is false, for one truth cannot contradict another. The philosopher will therefore bow, not indeed to the verdict of physics, but to the verdict of philosophy judging itself by means of physics, and will revise his arguments accordingly.)

[1] It is true, no doubt, that we have actually to do, not with philosophy, but with philosophers, and that philosophers are fallible, and a philosopher may therefore be mistaken in judging an hypothesis of physics, but this does not prove that he has no right to judge it.

A physicist may therefore be justified in a particular case in maintaining an hypothesis of physics against a philosopher who asserts that it contradicts a truth of philosophy. But that is because the evidence he possesses in support of his hypothesis convinces him that the philosopher is mistaken in his verdict—in other words, has not given it *ut philosophus*, as a mouthpiece of philosophy. But he would not therefore be justified in denying the philosopher's competence as such to determine the question.

[2] For example, when the philosophical doctrine of *free will* appears to the mechanists to contradict the physical law of the *conservation of energy*.

Moreover, since the laws of one science are subordinate to the laws of a superior science, it clearly follows that it is the office of the superior science to govern the inferior. But since the principles of philosophy (the first philosophy or metaphysics) are the absolutely first principles of all human knowledge, they possess an authority over the principles of all other human sciences, which are in a certain sense dependent upon them. That is to say, philosophy (the first philosophy or metaphysics) *governs* the other sciences.

Since the principles of philosophy (the first philosophy or metaphysics) are the absolutely first principles of all human knowledge, the principles or postulates of all human sciences are in a certain sense dependent upon them.

They do not, it is true, depend directly on the principles of metaphysics, as the truth of a conclusion depends on the truth of its premisses. They are self-evident by the light of natural reason (*principia per se nota*). But they are not absolutely speaking (*simpliciter*) first principles. Therefore, although they carry conviction independently of metaphysics, nevertheless they presuppose in fact the principles of metaphysics and can be resolved into them. They can be known without an explicit knowledge of the principles of metaphysics, but they could not be true, unless the latter were true. And in this sense they are indirectly subordinate to the latter. For instance, the mathematical axiom, *two quantities which are equal to a third quantity are equal to one another*, can be resolved into the metaphysical axiom of which it is a special case : *two beings identical with a third are identical with one another*.

It is for this reason that all the sciences are said to

be *indirectly subordinate* to metaphysics. Moreover, they are obliged on occasion to employ the universally valid principles of metaphysics. In this sense they are said to be subordinate to metaphysics in a particular aspect or relatively (*secundum quid*).

To govern or direct anything is to prescribe its object or end. The sciences are not directed by philosophy to their end, in the sense that they cannot attain it without the aid of philosophy. Arithmetic, for example, has no need of philosophy to investigate the numerical truths which it investigates of its very nature. Philosophy, however, assigns the distinctive ends of the special sciences in the sense that it determines speculatively the distinctive object of each, and what constitutes their specific unity and differentiation from the rest (classification of the sciences).[1] And so doing it assigns the order in which they stand one to another. Thus all the sciences are ordered by wisdom : *sapientis est ordinare*. If therefore a science, or more correctly a scientist, should happen to lose sight of its true object by encroaching on the domain and rights of another science,[2] it is the duty of philosophy to redress the disorder involved. In this capacity philosophy governs or directs the sciences

[1] A problem discussed in major logic.

[2] Such divagations and encroachments are only too frequent. For example, the non-Euclidean geometries may be so treated as to divert mathematics from its proper end. On the other hand, since Descartes, mathematics has usurped the domain of all the sciences, and in our time physics and chemistry are constantly encroaching upon the domain of biology, medicine upon psychology ; while the incursions made by physics or biology into the province of philosophy itself are innumerable : for example, the pseudo-scientific theories of the *non-existence of final causes*, the *unreality of qualities*, *determinism*, *atomism*, or the biological dogmas of *transformism* and *mechanism*.

(to these distinctive ends), not by positive prescription, but by setting them right, if they transgress their boundaries.

On the other hand, that knowledge in which the mind attains its ultimate good, that is to say, the highest knowledge, may be regarded as the common transcendent goal towards which all the special sciences converge. But this knowledge is bestowed by philosophy—the science of first causes—which in this capacity governs or directs the sciences in view of the common end to which their particular objects are subordinate. All the sciences are thus directed to wisdom.

From all we have just said it follows that to be proficient in the sciences it is not necessary to be a philosopher or to base one's work on a philosophy ; neither need the scientist while engaged in his special task seek advice from the philosopher or attempt to play the philosopher himself ; but " philosophy alone enables the man of science to understand the position and bearings of his special science in the sum-total of human knowledge " or " to acquire a notion either of the principles implicit in all experimental knowledge or the true foundations of the special sciences." [1] It follows, further, that a period in the history of human culture in which philosophy is not allowed her rightful suzerainty over the sciences as *scientia rectrix* [2] inevitably ends in a condition of intellectual chaos and a general weakening of the reasoning faculty.

Descartes, just because he absorbed all the sciences

[1] T. Richard, *Philosophie du raisonnement dans la science d'après Sain Thomas*, p. 14.
[2] St. Thomas, *In Metaph.*, Introduction.

in philosophy, and regarded science as absolutely and without qualification one, believed that the principles of all the sciences depend *directly* on the principles of the first philosophy (metaphysics). In consequence he held that the study of the sciences and of philosophy itself must begin with metaphysics, that is to say, with the coping-stone of the entire edifice.

The contrary error is the belief that the principles of science are *absolutely independent* of the principles of philosophy. There is therefore no place for a *scientia rectrix*, and the sciences are no longer a structure built on a definite plan, but a formless agglomeration. It is surprising that Auguste Comte, who wished to reduce philosophy to a mere systematisation of the special sciences, failed to see that this very function of classifying and systematising the sciences (in what he terms their *objective synthesis*) is only possible if philosophy is a distinct science of a higher order on which the others are in a certain respect dependent.[1]

Philosophy of Aristotle and St. Thomas

The principles of the special sciences are subordinate to the principles of philosophy, but only indirectly. Philosophy therefore governs the other sciences, but its government is such that it may be termed *constitutional*. (The special sciences are autonomous.) The study of the first philosophy (metaphysics) should be undertaken, not at the beginning, but at the end of intellectual research.

Philosophy of Descartes	Philosophy of those who reject Philosophy
The principles of the special sciences are directly subordinate to those of	The principles of the special sciences are not subordinate to the prin-

[1] For Comte, indeed, *sociology* takes the position of *scientia rectrix*, only, however, as ordering the sciences in reference to the human subject, not in themselves. (*Subjective synthesis.*)

philosophy. The latter therefore exercises over the other sciences a government which may be termed *despotic*.

The study of the first philosophy (metaphysics) should be undertaken at the beginning of intellectual research.

ciples of any science of a higher order. These sciences therefore are in no sense governed but are in a condition which may be termed *anarchy*. There is no supreme science or first philosophy (metaphysics).

Finally, if a science bases its demonstrations on certain postulates or data, which it can neither explain nor defend, there must be a superior science whose function it is to defend these postulates or data. In this sense the science of architecture defends that of building. It is, however, obvious that every science, except the highest, bases its demonstrations on postulates or data it is incapable of explaining or defending. For instance, mathematics does not inquire what is the nature of quantity, number, or extension, nor physics what is the nature of matter. And if an objector should deny that *the sensible world exists*, that *two quantities equal to a third are equal to one another*, or that *space has three dimensions*, neither physics nor mathematics can refute his objection, since they on the contrary assume these postulates or data. Therefore it must be the function of philosophy (the first philosophy or metaphysics) to *defend* against every possible objection the postulates of all the human sciences.

It is from common sense, or from the natural evidence of the intellect and experience, that the sciences derive their postulates. This is no doubt their sufficient warrant to build on these postulates, but it is insufficient to safeguard and protect them against errors which call the postulates in question. And it is also insufficient to provide for the perfecting stability and essential needs of human knowledge. Human knowledge would remain excessively imperfect and weak, and would fail to reach its final end, if the postulates of the sciences were not scientifically explained, discussed, and defended.

Philosophy, therefore, and particularly the first philosophy or metaphysics, because it is wisdom and the supreme science, judges, governs, and defends the other sciences. But the ruler is certainly not dependent upon those whom he governs. We therefore conclude that philosophy is independent of the inferior sciences, or at any rate depends on them only in the sense that a superior, when he is not strong enough to be self-sufficient, depends on the servants or instruments which he employs. It was for this reason that Aristotle regarded philosophy as the science pre-eminently *free*.

Philosophy appeals to the facts, the data of experience. To obtain the necessary materials it uses as instruments the truths provided by the evidence of the senses and the conclusions proved by the sciences. It depends on both, as a superior who cannot do his own work depends on the servants he employs.

A dependence of this kind is a purely material dependence, since the superior depends on the inferior to be served by him, not to do him service. He therefore judges by his own light of whatever his servants bring him to supply his needs. For example, one of the most successful students of bees, François

Huber, who was blind, interpreted by the light of his intellect the facts seen by his servants' eyes.

But further, this purely material dependence of philosophy, though absolutely necessary in respect of the evidence of the senses, is relative and contingent in respect to the conclusions of the sciences. It is in fact from the evidence of the senses that philosophy derives the fundamental principles which—interpreted by its own light—it employs as premisses in its demonstrations and as the means to prove its special truths. For instance, the truth, perceived by the senses and interpreted by the light of philosophy, *there is motion in the universe*, served Aristotle as the premiss from which he proved that being is divided into act and potentiality, and that there is a first mover that is pure act (God). It is obvious that philosophy is absolutely unable to dispense with data of this kind, and that the data thus employed as premisses must be absolutely true. Otherwise the conclusions which philosophy deduces from them would be uncertain. But it is otherwise with the propositions and conclusions of the sciences. No doubt these conclusions, if true, contribute to the store of materials utilised by philosophy—but philosophy (and particularly the first philosophy or metaphysics) is under no necessity to employ them, indeed ought not to employ them to establish its own conclusions, at any rate not its certain conclusions, though it may make use of them as confirmatory evidence. It must certainly have at its disposal some scientific conclusions, indeed as plentiful a supply as possible, because it cannot develop its principles satisfactorily until it sees them embodied, so to speak, in concrete examples which the senses can perceive. But it does not need one *particular* scientific proposition rather than any other, provided, that is to say, that, true to its own nature and maintaining the liberty due to a superior science, it draws its proofs from its own principles and from the fundamental truths supplied by the evidence of the senses and not from the conclusions supplied by the sciences. These latter, in fact, should not be premisses but simply illustrations which assist philosophy to attain its own truths. A sound philosophy can therefore dispense with the particular system of scientific explanations of which it makes use in accordance with the state of science at a particular epoch, and if that system were one day proved false the truth of that philosophy would not be affected. Only its language and the sensible illustrations with which it clothed its truths would require modification.

These remarks are important. They show how the datum of experience on which philosophy is primarily based suffices for the requirements of a supreme and universal science. This datum is provided by an instrument—the evidence of the senses—earlier than scientific observation, infinitely more certain than the inductions of the sciences, and placed by nature at the disposal of every man, and consists of truths so simple that they are universally and absolutely valid, so immediate and evident that their certainty exceeds that of the best established scientific conclusions.[1]

---

[1] To this fundamental datum we may add—but as secondary matter and at times valuable confirmation—the facts of a more special description discovered, controlled, and measured by the observations and experiments of science. We should bear in mind that the absolutely evident truths which constitute the primitive and fundamental datum of philosophy must be carefully distinguished from

From what has been said we can also understand why the purely scientific mistakes to be found in older statements of Aristotelian and Thomistic philosophy, statements which inevitably bear the stamp of the scientific beliefs of their period, do nothing to discredit the truth of that philosophy. For no philosophy has observed more faithfully than that of Aristotle and St. Thomas the laws of thought which guarantee its purity and freedom.

On the other hand philosophy, though distinct from the special sciences, is not unrelated to or isolated from them. On the contrary, it possesses the duty to exercise its office as *scientia rectrix* by constantly throwing its light on the discoveries and hypotheses, the unceasing activity and the development of the sciences, and one of the most essential requisites for its life and progress in the world is to maintain an intimate contact with the lower branches of study whose data it interprets and renders fruitful.

To the extent to which philosophy thus concerns itself with interpreting by the aid of its own truths the facts or hypotheses which positive science regards as proved, the errors or lacunae of positive science may introduce accidentally into a true system of philosophy elements of error which are, so to speak, the token and price of the human development of philosophy—but

certain interpretations of experience drawn from unscientific observation which are nothing more than pseudo-scientific statements. If, for example, in natural philosophy, to prove the reality of substantial change, it were argued that whereas water is a liquid body, hydrogen and oxygen are gaseous bodies, the argument would rest, not on a truth attested by the senses, but on a scientific error, for in reality the same inorganic bodies are found in the three states solid, liquid, and gaseous. Obviously an adequate scientific training helps the philosopher to avoid pitfalls of this kind.

they can only falsify a philosophy itself to the extent to which it is untrue to its own nature and enslaves itself to the lower branches of study.[1]

It is clear from everything which has been said that the nature and needs of philosophy make it incumbent upon the philosopher to keep himself as fully acquainted as he can with the scientific knowledge of his period, provided, however, that he preserves intact the freedom of philosophic truth. For though the philosopher as such need not use the affirmations of the special sciences to establish his own truths, he ought to make use of them, (i) to illustrate aptly his principles, (ii) to confirm his conclusions, (iii) to interpret, throw light upon, and assimilate, the assured results of the sciences so far as questions of philosophy are involved. And finally he should use the affirmations of science (iv) to refute objections and errors which claim support from its results.

From yet another point of view the study of the sciences is necessary for the philosopher : his own education must of necessity, owing to the very conditions of human nature, be a progress from the imperfect to the perfect, so that before undertaking the study of wisdom he should undergo the training of the sciences.[2]

---

[1] The " crime " of the decadent Scholastics of the sixteenth and seventeenth centuries was that they believed, and made others believe, that the philosophy of Aristotle and St. Thomas was in this sense bound up with the mistakes of ancient science, of which it is in reality wholly independent.

[2] The philosopher also requires a scientific training to be in a position to distinguish readily between the primary evidence of experience and certain popular but really pseudo-scientific interpretations of experience, such, for example, as the hypothesis of the sun's motion around the earth or the over-hasty belief that a particular inorganic body is essentially liquid and another essentially solid or gaseous.

It is not therefore surprising that all the great philosophers have been thoroughly acquainted with contemporary science. Some have even been great scientists (for example Aristotle, Albertus Magnus, and Leibniz), and several scientific discoveries of the first magnitude has been made by philosophers, for instance the mathematical discoveries of Pythagoras, Descartes, and Leibniz.

In this connection we may observe that a profound and practical knowledge of a single science with which the student is directly acquainted contributes far more to a philosophic training than a superficial and second-hand knowledge of a large number. Though owing to the degree to which specialisation has been carried in modern times he cannot hope ever to possess that complete knowledge of all the sciences which is possessed by the scientist in his particular department, the philosopher should nevertheless aim at acquiring a sufficiently thorough knowledge of the entire body of the sciences, an ideal in itself not beyond the bounds of possibility, as is proved by the example of several powerful minds.

Conclusion II.—Philosophy is the highest of all branches of human knowledge and is in the true sense wisdom. The other (human) sciences are subject to philosophy, in the sense that it judges and governs them and defends their postulates. Philosophy on the other hand is free in relation to the sciences, and only depends on them as the instruments which it employs.

VII

PHILOSOPHY AND THEOLOGY

PHILOSOPHY is the highest of the *human* sciences, that is, of the sciences which know things by the natural light of reason. But there is a science above it. For if there be a science whch is a participation by man of the knowledge proper to God himself, obviously that science will be superior to the highest human science. Such a science, however, exists; it is *theology*.

The word *theology* means the science of God. The science or knowledge of God which we can attain naturally by the unassisted powers of reason, and which enables us to know God by means of creatures as the author of the natural order, is a philosophic science—the supreme department of metaphysics—and is known as *theodicy* or *natural theology*. The knowledge or science of God which is unattainable naturally by the unassisted powers of reason, and is possible only if God has informed men about himself by a revelation from which our reason, enlightened by faith, subsequently draws the implicit conclusions, is *supernatural theology* or simply *theology*. It is of this science that we are now speaking.

Its object is something wholly inaccessible to the natural apprehension of any creature whatsoever, namely, God known in himself, in his own divine life, or in technical language *sub ratione Deitatis*, not, as in natural theology, God as the first cause of creatures and the author of the natural order. And all theological knowledge is knowledge in terms of God thus apprehended, whereas all metaphysical knowledge, including the metaphysical knowledge of God, is knowledge in terms of being in general.

The premisses of theology are the truths formally revealed by God (*dogmas* or articles of faith), and its primary criterion of truth the authority of God who reveals it.

Its light is no longer the more natural light of reason, but the light of reason illuminated by faith, *virtual revelation* in the language of theology, that is to say, revelation in so far as it implicitly (virtually) contains whatever conclusions reason can draw from it.

Alike by the sublimity of its object, the certainty of its premisses, and the excellence of its light, theology is above all merely human sciences. And although it is unable to perceive the truth of its premisses, which the theologian believes, whereas the premisses of philosophy are seen by the philosopher, it is nevertheless a science superior to philosophy. Though, as St. Thomas points out, the argument from authority is the weakest of all, where human authority is concerned, the argument from the authority of God, the revealer, is more solid and powerful than any other.[1]

And finally as the object of theology is he who is above all causes, it claims with a far better title than

---

[1] *Licet locus ab auctoritate, quae fundatur super ratione humana, sit infirmissimus, locus tamen ab auctoritate quae fundatur super revelatione divina est efficacissimus.* St. Thomas, *Sum. Theol.* i, q. 1, a 8, *ad* 2.

metaphysics the name of *wisdom*. It is wisdom *par excellence*.[1] What relations, then, must obtain between philosophy and theology?

As the superior science, theology *judges* philosophy in the same sense that philosophy judges the sciences.[2] It therefore exercises in respect of the latter a function of guidance or government, though a negative government, which consists in rejecting as false any philosophic affirmation which contradicts a theological truth. In this sense theology controls and exercises jurisdiction over the conclusions maintained by philosophers.

The *premisses* of philosophy, however, are independent of theology, being those primary truths which are self-evident to the understanding, whereas the premisses of theology are the truths revealed by God. The premisses of philosophy are self-supported and are not derived from those of theology. Similarly the light by which philosophy knows its object is independent

---

[1] Theology is theoretical wisdom, *par excellence* the wisdom which knows God by the intellect and its ideas, that is to say, by the normal processes of human knowledge. There is another wisdom of a still higher order which is a gift of the Holy Spirit, and enables us to know God experimentally and by means of charity. It enables us to judge of divine things instinctively, as the virtuous man judges of virtue (*per modum inclinationis*), not scientifically as the moralist judges of virtue (*per modum cognitionis*). *Cf.* St. Thomas, *Sum. Theol.* i, q. 1, a 6, *ad* 3.

[2] See above, pp. 111 *sqq.* The philosopher and the scientist are never entitled to deny the rights which theology possesses over philosophy and the sciences. They may, however, be justified in rejecting in a particular instance, not indeed the authority of the Church, but the judgment of an individual theologian, since the individual theologian does not necessarily speak as the mouthpiece of theology, and may therefore be mistaken.

of theology, since its light is the light of *reason*, which is its own guarantee.[1] For these reasons philosophy is not positively governed by theology,[2] nor has it any need of theology to defend its premises (whereas it defends those of the other sciences). It develops its principles autonomously within its own sphere, though subject to the external control and negative regulation of theology.

It is therefore plain that philosophy and theology are entirely distinct, and that it would be as absurd for a philosopher to invoke the authority of revelation to prove a philosophical thesis as for a geometrician to attempt to prove a theorem by the aid of physics, for example, by weighing the figures he is comparing. But if philosophy and theology are entirely distinct, they are not therefore unrelated, and although philosophy is of all the human sciences pre-eminently the free science, in the sense that it proceeds by means of premises and laws which depend on no science superior to itself, its freedom—that is, its freedom to err—is limited in so far as it is subject to theology, which controls it externally.

In the seventeenth century the Cartesian reform

[1] This light is its own evidence and in philosophy is sufficient of itself. But this does not prevent it serving also—in theology, however, not in philosophy—as the instrument of a superior light ; neither, of course, does it imply that human reason is not subordinate in its very principles to the First Intellect.

[2] Theology can turn the investigations of philosophy in one direction rather than in another, in which case it may be said to regulate philosophy positively by accident (*per accidens*). But absolutely speaking theology can regulate philosophy only negatively, as has been explained above. Positively it does not regulate it either directly, by furnishing its proofs (as faith for apologetics), or indirectly, by classifying its divisions (as philosophy itself classifies the sciences).

resulted in the severance of philosophy from theology,[1] the refusal to recognise the rightful control of theology and its function as a negative rule in respect of philosophy. This was tantamount to denying that theology is a science, or anything more than a mere practical discipline, and to claiming that philosophy, or human wisdom, is the absolutely sovereign science, which admits no other superior to itself. Thus, in spite of the religious beliefs of Descartes himself, Cartesianism introduced the principle of *rationalist* philosophy, which denies God the right to make known by revelation truths which exceed the natural scope of reason. For if God has indeed revealed truths of this kind, human reason enlightened by faith will inevitably employ them as premisses from which to obtain further knowledge and thus form a science, theology. And if theology is a science, it must exercise in respect of philosophy the function of a negative rule, since the same proposition cannot be true in philosophy, false in theology.[2]

[1] It may, it is true, be replied that Descartes's intention was simply to emancipate philosophy from the authority of a particular theological system—Scholasticism—which he regarded as worthless, because it took its philosophic or metaphysical principles from Aristotle.

In reality, however, it was with theology itself that he broke, when he broke with Scholasticism, which is the traditional theology of the Church. And moreover his conception of science implied the denial of his scientific value of theology. In any case the result of his reform was the assertion of the absolute independence of philosophy in relation to theology. (*Cf.* Blondel, " Le Christianisme de Descartes." *Revue de Métaph. et de Morale*, 1896.)

[2] The theory of a double truth, by which the same thing may be true in philosophy, but false in theology, was invented by the mediaeval Averroists, who sought in this way to evade the censures of the Church. In various forms it has been revived in modern times by all who, like the modernists, wish to keep the name of Catholics while freely professing in philosophy opinions destructive of some particular dogmatic truth.

On the other hand, philosophy renders to theology services of the greatest value where it is employed by the latter. For in fact theology employs in its demonstrations truths proved by philosophy. Philosophy thus becomes the instrument of theology, and it is in this respect and in so far as it serves theological argument that it is called *ancilla theologiae*. In itself, however, and when it is proving its own conclusions, it is not a bond-servant but free, subject only to the external control and negative ruling of theology.

As was shown above, philosophy is from the very nature of things obliged to employ as an instrument the evidence of the senses, and even, in a certain fashion, the conclusions of the special sciences. Theology, considered in itself as a science subordinate to the knowledge of God and the blessed, is not in this way obliged to make use of philosophy, but is absolutely independent.

In practice, however, on account of the nature of its possessor, that is to say, on account of the weakness of the human understanding, which can reason about the things of God only by analogy with creatures, it cannot be developed without the assistance of philosophy. But the theologian does not stand in the same relation to philosophy as the philosopher to the sciences.[1] We have seen above that the philosopher

[1] This distinction between the relationship of theology to philosophy and that of philosophy to the special sciences derives from the fact that, since theology is a participation of the divine wisdom, the human subject is too weak for its unaided study and to draw conclusions from it is compelled to employ as premisses conclusions established by an inferior discipline.

Since, however, philosophy is a human wisdom, at which reason can

should employ the propositions or conclusions which he borrows from the sciences, not to establish his own conclusions (at any rate not conclusions for which metaphysical certainty is claimed), but merely to illustrate his principles, and therefore that the truth of a metaphysical system does not depend on the truth of the scientific material it employs. The theologian, on the contrary, makes use at every turn of philosophic propositions to prove his own conclusions. Therefore a system of theology could not possibly be true if the metaphysics which it employed were false. It is indeed an absolute necessity that the theologian should have at his disposal a true philosophy in conformity with the common sense of mankind.

Philosophy taken in itself normally precedes theology. Certain fundamental truths of the natural order are indeed what we may term the introduction to the faith (*praeambula fidei*). These truths, which are naturally known to all men by the light of common sense, are known and proved scientifically by philosophy. Theology, being the science of faith, presupposes the philosophical knowledge of these same truths.

Philosophy considered as the instrument of theology serves the latter, principally in three ways. In the first place theology employs philosophy to prove the truths which support the foundations of the faith in that department of theology which is termed apolo-

arrive, though with difficulty, by its unassisted natural power, the human mind should be able to draw from it certain conclusions (especially metaphysically certain conclusions) without employing as premisses the conclusions of sciences to which it is superior in dignity and in certainty.

getics,[1] which shows, for example, how miracles prove the divine mission of the Church; secondarily to impart some notion of the mysteries of faith by the aid of analogies drawn from creatures—as for instance when theology uses the philosophic conception of *verbum mentale*, the mental word,[2] to illustrate the dogma of the Trinity; and finally to refute the adversaries of the faith—as when theology shows by means of the philosophic theory of *quantity*[3] that the mystery of the Eucharist is in no way opposed to reason.

We must not forget that, if philosophy serves theology, it receives in return valuable assistance from the latter.

In the first place, so far as it is of its nature subject to the external control and negative ruling of theology, it is protected from a host of errors; and if its freedom to err is thus restricted, its freedom to attain truth is correspondingly safeguarded.[4]

In the second place, in so far as it is the instrument of theology, it is led to define more precisely and with more subtle refinements important concepts and theories which, left to itself, it would be in danger of neglecting. For example, it was under the influence

[1] See Garrigou-Lagrange, *De Revelatione*, i, 2, 1918.
[2] A theory studied in psychology.
[3] An explanation given by cosmology.
[4] Unassisted reason can indeed avoid error on any particular point whatsoever within the sphere of philosophy, but in view of the weakness of human nature it is unable without the assistance of grace to avoid error on some point or other; that is to say, without a special grace or the negative control of revelation and theology it cannot achieve a perfect human wisdom. (*Cf.* St. Thomas, *Sum. Theol.*, i, q. 1, a. 1; *Sum. contra Gent.*, i, 4; Garrigou-Lagrange, *De Rev.*, i, pp. 411 *sqq.*)

of theology that Thomism elaborated the theory of *nature* and *personality*, and perfected the theory of the *habitus*, habits, etc.

Conclusion III.—Theology, or the science of God so far as He has been made known to us by revelation, is superior to philosophy. Philosophy is subject to it, neither in its premises nor in its method, but in its conclusions, over which theology exercises a control, thereby constituting itself a negative rule of philosophy.

VIII

BEFORE we know things with a scientific or perfect knowledge by reflecting upon them and by their causes, we know them imperfectly (*unscientific knowledge*, the knowledge of everyday life). We must remember that we are obliged not only to begin with this unscientific knowledge of everyday life ; we must be content with it to the end, improving it more or less by study and reading, in that enormous number of cases where science in the strict sense is unattainable.

For, so far as the knowledge of secondary causes is concerned, no man can possibly attain, with the perfection required of the genuine scientist, universal knowledge ; in other words, he cannot specialise in all branches of science, a contradiction in terms. He is fortunate, indeed, if he can make himself master of a single science. For all the others he must be satisfied with a knowledge which, however enriched and improved it may be in the case of what is known as a cultivated man, that is to say, a man well acquainted with the scientific knowledge of other people, is always inferior to science in the strict sense. But in the domain of first causes, the science of all things is within a man's grasp, for it is precisely the distinguishing character of the science called philosophy to know all things by their first causes,[1] and it is to the philosopher or the sage, the wise man, that we have the right to apply Leonardo da Vinci's aphorism : *facile cósa e farsi universale* ; it is easy for a man to make himself universal.

Ordinary knowledge consists for the most part of mere opinions or beliefs, more or less well founded. But it implies a solid kernel of genuine *certainties* in which the philosopher recognises in the first place data of the senses (for example, that *bodies possess length, breadth, and height*), secondly, self-evident axioms (for example, *the whole is greater than the part, every event has a cause*, etc.), and thirdly, consequences immediately deducible from these axioms (proximate conclusions). These certainties which arise spontaneously in the mind when we first come to the use of reason are thus the work of nature in us, and may therefore be called an endowment of nature [2] as proceeding from the natural perception, consent, instinct, or natural sense of the intellect. Since their source is human nature itself, they will be found in all men alike ; in other words, they are common to all men. They may therefore be said to belong to the common perception, consent, or instinct, or to the *common sense* of mankind.

The great truths without which man's moral life is impossible—for example, knowledge of God's existence, the freedom of the will, etc.—belong to this domain of

[1] It is therefore obvious what a stupendous delusion is involved in the positivist view of philosophy. Were philosophy merely the co-ordination or systematisation of the sciences, its attainment would presuppose a perfect mastery of all the sciences, that is to say, specialisation in every science, which amounts to saying that philosophy is beyond the reach of man.

[2] Kleutgen, *La philosophie scolastique*, i, p. 439.

common sense, as consequences immediately deducible (proximate conclusions) from primary data apprehended by observation and first principles apprehended by the intellect. All men, unless spoiled by a faulty education or by some intellectual vice, possess a natural certainty of these truths. But those whose understanding has never been cultivated are not able to give any account or at least any satisfactory account of their convictions ; that is to say, they cannot explain why they possess them.

These certainties of common sense, conclusions of an implicit reasoning, are as well founded as the certainties of science. But their possessor has no knowledge, or an imperfect knowledge, of the grounds on which he bases them. They are therefore imperfect not in their value as truth but in the *mode* or condition under which they exist in the mind.

Of the self-evident truths (*the whole is greater than the part, every event has a cause*, etc.) which are the object of what is termed *the understanding of principles*, and whose certainty is superior to that of any conclusion of science, common sense possesses a knowledge whose mode is equally imperfect, because it is confused and implicit.

Common sense therefore may be regarded as the natural and primitive judgment of human reason, infallible, but imperfect in its mode.

The wholly spontaneous character of common sense, and its inability to give an account of its convictions, have led certain philosophers to regard it as a special faculty purely instinctive and unrelated to the intellect (the Scottish school, end of eighteenth and beginning of nineteenth century ; Reid, Dugald Stewart, and in France, Jouffroy), or as a sentiment distinct from and superior to reason (the intuitive or sentimentalist school ; for instance, Rousseau, Jacobi, and in our own time Bergson). But in that case it would necessarily be blind, for we possess no other light than that of the intellect or reason. The light of common sense is fundamentally the same light as that of science, that is to say, the natural light of the intellect. But in common sense this light does not return upon itself by critical reflection, and is not perfected by what we shall learn to know as a *scientific habit* (*habitus*).

We must now define the relations which obtain between philosophy and common sense.

Philosophy cannot, as the Scottish school maintained, be founded on the authority of common sense understood simply as the *common consent* or universal witness of mankind, or as an instinct which in fact compels our assent. For it is in fact founded on evidence, not on authority of any kind.

But if by common sense we understand only *the immediate apprehension of self-evident first principles*, which is one of its constituents, we may say with truth that it is the source of the whole of philosophy. For the premisses of philosophy are indeed the evident axioms which in virtue of its natural constitution implant in the mind its primary certainties.

It is important to be quite clear that, if philosophy finds its premisses already enunciated by common sense, it accepts them not because they are enunciated by common sense, or on the authority of common sense understood as the universal consent or common instinct of mankind, but entirely and solely on the authority of the *evidence*.

Finally, if we take into account the entire body of truths (premisses and conclusions) known by common sense with certainty but in an imperfect mode, we must conclude that philosophy is superior to common sense, as the perfect stage of anything (in this case the scientific stage of knowledge) is superior to the imperfect or rudimentary stage of the same thing (in this case the pre-scientific stage of the same knowledge, which is yet true and certain at both stages).

If in common sense we consider not the conclusions which it reaches but the premisses alone, it is still inferior to philosophy in respect of its *mode* of knowledge, but superior alike to philosophy and to all the sciences in respect of its *object* and of the *light* in which it knows. For, as we have said above, philosophy and all the sciences are ultimately founded on the natural evidence of first principles (to which philosophy returns—in criticism—to study them scientifically, whereas the other sciences are content to accept them from nature).

Philosophy studies scientifically the three categories of truths to which common sense bears instructive witness : (i) the truths of fact which represent the evidence of the senses ; (ii) the self-evident first principles of the understanding, in as much as it clears up their meaning by critical reflection and defends them rationally ; (iii) the consequences immediately deducible (proximate conclusions) from these first principles, inasmuch as it provides a rational proof of them. And, further, where common sense yields to the mere opinions of popular belief, philosophy continues to extend indefinitely the domain of scientific certainty. Thus philosophy *justifies* and continues common sense, as, for instance, the art of poetry justifies and continues the natural rhythms of language.

It is also the province of philosophy to decide what are the genuine certainties affirmed by common sense, and what is their true significance ; a function which common sense is incapable of performing, for the very reason that it does not understand, or does not understand clearly, the grounds of its knowledge. In this sense philosophy *controls* common sense, as, for example, the art of poetry controls the natural rhythms of language.

Nevertheless, common sense has the right and duty to reject any philosophic teaching which denies a truth of which it possesses natural certainty, as the inferior has the right and duty to oppose a superior who acts in a manner evidently unjust. For as soon as a truth becomes known to us, by whatever channel, it is a sin not to accept it. Common sense may therefore *accidentally judge* philosophy.

It is related of Diogenes that when Zeno the Eleatic was arguing in his presence against the possibility of motion, his sole reply was to get up and walk. Similarly, when Descartes taught that motion is relative or " reciprocal," so that it makes no difference whether you say the moving object is moving towards the goal or the goal towards the moving object, the English philosopher Henry More retorted that when a man runs towards a goal panting and tiring himself,[1] he has no doubt which of the two, the moving object or the goal, is in motion.

These protests of common sense based on the evidence of the senses were perfectly justified. It must, however, be added that they were insufficient

[1] Letter of March 5, 1649.

—not indeed to confute the respective theses of Zeno and Descartes but to confute them as errors in philosophy. That would have demanded a philosophic refutation of the arguments adduced by these philosophers, and explanations showing why and at what point they went wrong.

It must be observed that though in itself and in order to establish its demonstrations philosophy does not depend upon the authority of common sense, understood as the universal consent or common instinct of mankind, nevertheless it is dependent upon it in a certain sense (*materially*, or in respect of the subject), in its origin as a human activity and in its development in the mind of philosophers. From this point of view philosophy may be compared to a building, and the great pre-scientific conclusions of common sense (the existence of God, the freedom of the will, etc.) to the scaffolding which nature has erected beforehand. Once the edifice has been completed it supports itself on its rock-bed, the natural self-evidence of its first principles, and has no need of scaffolding. But without the scaffolding it could not have been built.

It is now evident how unreasonable that philosophy is, which priding itself on its scientific knowledge of things despises common sense *a priori* and on principle, and cuts itself off from its natural convictions. Descartes (who in other respects and in his very conception of science concedes too much to common sense) began this divorce, on the one hand, by admitting as the only certain truths those scientifically established, thus denying the intrinsic value of the convictions of common sense, and on the other hand, by professing as part of his system several doctrines incompatible with those convictions. His disciple Malebranche, and above all the *critical* philosophers of the Kantian school, as also certain *modernist* philosophers, have carried this tendency to its extreme, until for some of these philosophers it is sufficient that a proposition should be acceptable to common sense for it to be questioned or denied by science, which would be contaminated by the " credulity " of the common herd, unless it taught the contrary of what mankind at large believes to be true.

Yet the greater the natural strength of a man's intelligence, the stronger should be his grasp of these natural certainties. He therefore who professes to condemn common sense shows not the strength but the weakness of his understanding.

It is now obvious that in its attitude to common sense, as in its solution of the majority of the great philosophic problems, Thomism keeps the golden mean between two opposing errors like a mountain summit between two valleys.

Philosophy of Aristotle and St. Thomas

The convictions of common sense are valid, and science is untrue to itself if it rejects them. But the basis of philosophy is the natural witness of the intellect, not the authority of common sense.

Scottish School

Not only are the convictions of common sense valid, but the authority of common sense imposing itself as a blind instinct on the mind is the foundation on which philosophy should be based.

Rationalist, Critical, and Modernist Schools

Not only is the authority of common sense incapable of furnishing the basis of philosophy, but the convictions of common sense are destitute of any speculative value.

From all that has been said it is evident what an important part the certainties of common sense play as an introduction to philosophy. Those who are beginning the study of philosophy and about to acquaint themselves with the most recent problems, and even perhaps the most misleading systems, ought to repose an absolute trust in the convictions of common sense of which they find their minds already possessed, for they will help them to rise to a higher and more perfect knowledge, conclusions scientifically established.

> *Conclusion IV.*—Philosophy is not based upon the authority of common sense understood as the universal consent or common instinct of mankind ; it is nevertheless derived from common sense considered as the understanding of self-evident first principles.
>
> It is superior to common sense as the perfect or " scientific " stage of knowledge is superior to the imperfect or ordinary stage of the same knowledge. Nevertheless philosophy may be accidentally judged by common sense.

For the purposes of this present outline we need only add that philosophy is not constructed *a priori* on the basis of some particular fact selected by the philosopher (Descartes's *cogito*), or principle arbitrarily laid down by him (Spinoza's *substance*, Fichte's *pure ego*, Schelling's *absolute*, Hegel's *idea*) whose consequences he ingeniously develops. Its formal principles are the first principles apprehended in the concept of being, whose cogency consists wholly in their evidence for the intellect,[1] and on the other hand its matter is experience, and its facts [2] the simplest and most obvious facts—the starting-point from which it rises to the causes and grounds which constitute the ultimate explanation. Not a whimsy spun out of his own brain, but the entire universe with its enormous multitude and variety of data must be the philosopher's teacher.

And he must always bear in mind that, if philosophy enables the human intellect to apprehend with absolute certainty the highest and most profound realities of the natural order, it cannot therefore claim to exhaust those realities by making them known to the utmost extent of their intelligibility. From this point of view science does not destroy the *mystery* of things, that in them which is still unknown and unfathomed, but on the contrary recognises and delimits it ; [3] even what it knows it never knows completely. The wise man knows all things, inasmuch as he knows them in their ultimate causes, but he does not know, is infinitely removed from knowing, everything about everything. Ignorance, however, is not the same as error. It is sufficient for the philosopher that he knows with

[1] This is what the *Positivists* fail to see.

[2] This is what the *pure intellectualists*—from Parmenides to Hegel—who construct their metaphysics wholly *a priori*, have failed to grasp.

[3] Aristotle (*Metaph.*, i, 2) remarks that the occasional cause of philosophy is τὸ θαυμάζειν, *admiratio*, by which he means wonder mingled with dread, in other words *awe*, a wonder which knowledge tends to remove. But we must be careful to understand his meaning of the wonder which does not understand, not of the admiration, indeed the awe, born of understanding. The wise man is astonished at nothing because he knows the ultimate causes of all things, but he admires far more than the ignorant man. *Cf. De Part. Anim.*, i, 5, 645 a 16 : ἐν πᾶσι τοῖς φυσικοῖς ἔνεστί τι θαυμαστόν.

certainty what it is his province to know and what it is of the first importance for us to know. Indeed, it is better not to know things which divert the mind from the highest knowledge, as Tacitus remarks : *nescire quaedam, magna pars sapientiae.*

*   *   *   *   *

We have considered the nature of philosophy ; it remains to distinguish its departments. We shall thus obtain a clear notion of its sphere, and at the same time become acquainted with its principal problems.

PART TWO

THE CLASSIFICATION OF PHILOSOPHY

K

I

THE MAIN DIVISIONS OF PHILOSOPHY

When a man undertakes a work, he begins by testing his tool in various ways to learn the use he can and should make of it.

The philosopher's work is to acquire knowledge ; his tool, reason. Therefore the philosopher before he begins his work must examine reason to discover the use he should make of it.

The study of reason as an instrument of acquiring knowledge or means of discovering truth is called *logic*.

Logic is therefore, strictly speaking, not so much a department of philosophy as a science or art, of which philosophy (and indeed all the sciences) makes use, and the introduction to philosophy. It is a *propaedeutic* to science.[1] The other sciences are dependent upon logic inasmuch as it teaches the method of procedure in the acquisition of knowledge, and we are obliged to possess the means or tools of knowledge before we can acquire knowledge itself.

It is thus evident that the study of philosophy must

---

[1] " *Res autem de quibus est logica, non quaeruntur ad cognoscendum propter seipsas, sed ut adminiculum quoddam ad alias scientias. Et ideo logica non continetur sub philosophia speculativa quasi principalis pars*, sed quasi quoddam reductum ad eam, *prout ministrat speculationi sua instrumenta, scilicet syllogismos et definitiones, et alia hujusmodi, quibus in speculativis scientiis indigemus. Unde et secundum Boethium in* Comment. sup. Porphyrium, *non tam est scientia quam* scientiae instrumentum." St. Thomas, *Sup. Boet. de Trin.*, q. 5, a. 1, *ad* 2. It is therefore only reductively that logic belongs to theoretical philosophy.

from the very nature of things begin with logic, although on account of its difficulty and extremely abstract character logic usually repels rather than attracts beginners.[1] A few of the moderns rebel against this order of study, and maintain that logic should be studied only in the course of learning the other branches of philosophy, or after they have been learned. But this is like arguing that the surgeon should only study anatomy by the practice or after the practice of his art upon the sick. It is absurd, Aristotle remarks, to study at the same time a science and its conditions or method of procedure. ἄτοπον ἅμα ζητεῖν ἐπιστήμην καὶ τρόπον ἐπιστήμης.[2]

When by the study of logic he has made himself master of his tool, the philosopher can set to work. What that work is we know already : to acquire a knowledge of things by their first principles.

If, however, we consider the aim of learning, there are two distinct types of knowledge. We can, for example, make use of our eyes simply in order to see

[1] *Cf.* St. Thomas, *Sup. Boet. de Trin.*, q. 6, a. 1, *ad* 3. "*Dicendum quod in addiscendo incipimus ab eo, quod est magis facile, nisi necessitas aliud requirat. Quandoque enim necesse est in addiscendo non incipere ab eo quod est facilius, sed ab eo a cujus cognitione cognitio sequentium dependet. Et hac positione oportet in addiscendo incipere a logica, non quia ipsa sit facilior scientiis ceteris ; habet enim maximam difficultatem, cum sit de secundo intellectis ; sed quia aliae scientiae ab ipsa dependent, in quantum ipsa docet modum procedendi in omnibus scientiis. Oportet enim primum scire modum scientiae quam scientiam ipsam, ut dicitur II. Metaph.*

[2] *Metaph.*, ii, 995 a 12. St. Thomas, *In II Metaph.*, l. 5. "*Quia enim diversi secundum diversos modos veritatem inquirunt, ideo oportet quod homo instruatur per quem modum in singulis scientiis sint recipienda ea quae dicuntur. Et quia non est facile, quod homo simul duo capiat, sed dum ad duo attendit, neutrum capere potest : absurdum est, quod homo simul quaerat scientiam et modum qui convenit scientiae. Et propter hoc debet prius addiscere logicam quam alias scientias, quia logica tradit communem modum procedendi in omnibus scientiis.*"

and enjoy the sight of things, and we can also make use of them for the practical purposes of life.

In the same way we can employ our reason scientifically, solely for the pleasure of knowledge. The sciences thus acquired exist *solely for the sake of knowledge* (the theoretical sciences). And if there be a theoretical science which seeks to account for things by their first principles, its object will be that which is the first principle in the theoretical order, namely, *the first causes* of everything which exist (that is to say, the first causes naturally knowable). That science is *theoretical philosophy*. We can, on the other hand, employ our reason scientifically for our profit and the improvement of our life ; the sciences thus acquired exist *to procure by some kind of activity the good of man* (the practical sciences). And if there be a practical science which seeks to regulate human acts by first principles, its object will be that which is the first principle in the practical order, namely, *the absolute good of man* (the absolute good naturally knowable).[1] Such a science is *practical philosophy*—otherwise termed moral science or *ethics*.[2]

There are, indeed, other practical sciences besides ethics ; for example, *medicine*, which seeks to procure the health of man. But the object of these sciences is not good, pure and simple (the sovereign good), but some particular human good. They do not,

[1] That is to say, the sovereign good of man as it would be, if his end were simply natural happiness. See below, pp. 265–267.

[2] Observe that this division of philosophy into theoretical and practical relates to the *end*, the aim, not to the object itself of the science, which as such is always necessarily theoretical. Therefore it does not enter into the specification in the strict sense of the philosophic sciences. See below, p. 271.

therefore, refer in the practical order to which they belong to the first principle of action, and for that reason are not philosophies. Ethics, or moral science, is thus the only practical science which deserves the name of philosophy.[1]

We must bear in mind that although the object of ethics is to procure a good which is not solely a good of the intellect, that is to say, does not consist in knowledge alone, its rule of truth is that which is, and it proceeds by way of demonstration, resolving conclusions into their premisses. In other words it is practical in virtue of its object (to know in order to procure the good of man in the ordering of his acts), but as science in the strict sense it is theoretical knowledge.[2]

We must further remark that the practical sciences are obviously subordinate to the theoretical, (i) as presupposing (if not in the order of their origin in

---

[1] It may be added that of the practical sciences, only one, ethics, is in fact *vere et proprie scientia*, that is to say, proceeds by way of demonstration, in a necessary matter, and imparts a truth, which consists in knowing things in conformity with what is, and not in properly directing a contingent action. The other practical sciences (medicine, architecture, strategy, etc.) are arts, not sciences in the strict sense. (*Cf.* John of St. Thomas, *Cursus Philos.*, i, *Log.* ii, q. 1, a. 5).

But though ethics is in the strict sense a science, it is for that very reason only in an indirect sense practical : for its procedure consists in providing knowledge (*speculabiliter*) not in producing action (*operabiliter*), and though it certainly supplies rules immediately applicable to concrete cases, the right application and good use of these rules in practice is the effect not of ethics but of the virtue of *prudence*.

On the other hand, as we shall see later, the philosophy of art is also, in a sense, a practical philosophy. But it is very far from being a practical science, even like ethics in the indirect sense, for it treats only of principles and is unable to descend to the rules immediately applicable to the concrete work to be executed.

[2] Hence even *practical* philosophy is a theoretical wisdom which proceeds by way of knowledge (see above, p. 102).

time, at least in the nature of things) the truths proved by these sciences, which they apply for the benefit of man—for example, medicine, as the science of healing, presupposes anatomy ; (ii) as sciences inferior in dignity to the theoretical sciences. For the latter are studied for their own sake, and are therefore good in themselves, whereas the practical sciences are studied for the good or utility of man, and are therefore good only in relation to that good or utility. It follows that philosophy in the strictest sense is theoretical philosophy (especially the first philosophy or *metaphysics*), logic being the science introductory to it, and ethics the science detached from it to treat specially of that which concerns the good of man.

We are now in a position to define more exactly the object of these three main divisions of philosophy.

A science which seeks to procure man's sovereign good must before all else treat of those things which are the indispensable conditions of its attainment. But these are the actions which man performs in the free exercise of his faculties ; in other words, human acts as such. We may therefore say that *human acts* are the formal object (subject-matter) of moral philosophy.

A science whose aim is to know things by their first causes must treat primarily of that in things which depends immediately upon those causes. But that in things which depends immediately upon the first or highest causes is that which is most essential in them, their being, and that which is the most widely, indeed universally, distributed, being, which everything whatsoever possesses. We therefore conclude that the formal object of theoretical philosophy is the *being* of things.

Now theoretical philosophy studies the being of things in different fashions and from higher or lower points of view (degrees of abstraction). It may study the being of things with their sensible properties (*ens mobile*), or the being of things with the sole properties of quantity (*ens quantum*), or the being of things with the sole properties of being (being *qua* being, *ens in quantum ens*). Hence arise the three principal divisions of theoretical philosophy (see below, Chs. III & IV).

Finally, a science which studies reason as the tool for the attainment of truth must treat before all else of that which we handle or manipulate when we reason. But that which we handle or manipulate when we reason is the *things* themselves. For example, when we affirm that *man is superior to the other animals because he possesses intellect*, it is indeed the thing itself, man, which we hold in our mind and to which we join or attribute those other things, intellect and superiority. But the man that we thus handle in our mind is obviously not the man as he exists, or can exist in reality; there is no question of seizing some man who passes in the street to stick an attribute on to his back. That our mind may work on them, things possess in the mind a manner of being which they do not and cannot possess in reality. They exist there *so far as they are known*. Predicated one of another divided, reunited, linked together according to the necessities of knowledge, they lead there a distinct life, with its own laws. It is this life and its laws, the order to which things must submit so far as they are objects of knowledge, if they are to guide the mind to truth, that logic primarily studies, and since it is concerned with something which exists and can exist only in the mind or with what philosophers term an *ens rationis*, a conceptual being, we may say that the formal object of logic is that conceptual being, *ens rationis* (the order which should prevail among conceptual objects) which directs the mind to truth.

As opposed to *conceptual being*, the *ens rationis*, which can exist only in the mind—for example, the *genus* animal or the *species* man (*the* genus *animal comprises mankind and the brutes*, man is the species *of Peter*)—we term *real being*, *ens reale*, that which exists or can exist in reality—for example, animals, man, human nature (*all animals are mortal, human nature is fallible*).

> *Conclusion V.*—Philosophy is divided into three principal parts : (i) *logic*, which is the introduction to philosophy in the strict sense, and which studies the conceptual being (*ens rationis*) which directs the mind to truth ; (ii) *theoretical philosophy* or simply philosophy, which studies the being of things (real being, *ens reale*) ; (iii) *practical philosophy* or ethics, which studies *human acts*.

II

LOGIC

Logic studies reason as the tool of knowledge. To study any complicated machine, a reaper for instance, we must begin by making it work in the void, while we learn how to use it correctly and without damaging it. In the same way we must first of all learn how to use *reason correctly*, that is to say, in conformity with the nature of ratiocination, and without damaging it. Hence arises our first problem : What are the rules which we must obey in order to reason correctly?

We should next study our reaper no longer in the void, but as applied to the actual material with which it was designed to deal, learning how to use it, not only correctly, but *profitably and efficiently*. In the same way we must study reasoning as applied to facts, asking ourselves under what conditions reasoning is not only correct but also true and conclusive, and productive of knowledge. It is in this department of logic that we study the methods employed by the different sciences. But before this a far graver problem will arise and demand solution.

It is by our *ideas* that things are presented to the mind, so that we can reason about them and acquire knowledge.

Everybody knows by experience what an idea is. It is sufficient for a man to reflect on what is in his mind, when he makes a judgment of any kind. For instance, *philosophers have made many mistakes ; philosophers, mistakes, have made, many*—all these are present in the mind as so many ideas. Nevertheless to clear up any possible obscurity, we will try to describe what everybody means by the word. We will, for instance, define ideas as images or interior reproductions of things, by which the latter are presented to us in such a way that we can reason about them (and thus acquire knowledge).

No doubt the words we employ express our ideas. But they bring with them something besides. If, for example, I pronounce the word *angel*, I have in my consciousness two images of the being in question. In the first place an idea, in virtue of which, strictly speaking, I know that particular being (the idea of a pure spirit), but in addition a *sensible representation* (the *image* of some figure more or less nebulous and winged) which possesses no likeness whatever to the being in question, for a purely spiritual being is invisible.

If, again, I pronounce the word *square* I have in my consciousness the idea of the square, by means of which I can reason about the thing concerned (the idea of a *rectangular polygon of four equal sides*) and at the same time a sensible representation—which in this case adequately represents the thing in question—a particular figure which I imagine drawn in chalk on the blackboard. The idea and the representation are quite distinct, as is shown by the fact that I can vary the latter in a host of different ways (the imaginary drawing can be larger or smaller, white, red, yellow, etc.) without any variation of the former. Moreover, if I were to pronounce, for example, the word *myriagon* instead of *square*, I should possess as definite and as clear an idea of it as I had of the square (the idea of *a polygon of ten thousand sides*), whereas the only sensible representation I could form of it would be extremely vague and confused.

It is evident that if the sensible representations assist me to reason, they are not the instrument with which I reason to acquire a knowledge of things. For I can reason as accurately about the *angel* or the *myriagon* as I can about the *square*. And my reasoning is in no way dependent on the thousand alterations I can make in my sensible representations of an *angel*, *myriagon*, or *square*.

From this we conclude that things are presented to our consciousness in two different fashions, either *by an idea* or *by a sensible representation*.

By the first we *think* (*intelligimus*) the thing, by the second we *imagine* it. The representation is simply a species of phantom, an image of what we have previously seen, heard, touched, etc., in short, of what has been originally made known to us by a sensation. Formerly called a *phantasm*, it is now called simply an *image*. In future, then, we shall reserve to denote it the term *image*, whose meaning we accordingly restrict. (But we must no longer use the same word to denote an idea.) We conclude, therefore, that—

Conclusion VI.—Ideas are the internal likenesses of things by which the latter are presented in such a way that we can reason about them (and thus acquire knowledge) ; images are the internal likenesses of things by which the latter are presented to us as our sensations have first made them known to us. Words directly signify ideas, at the same time evoking images.

If now we compare objects as they are presented by ideas and as they are presented by sensations or images, we see at once that they are distinguished by a character of the very first importance. If, for example, I call up before my mind the image of a man, I see present in my imagination with outlines more or less vague and more or less simplified some particular man. He is fair or dark, tall or short, white or black, etc. But if I form the idea of man, as, for instance, when I state the proposition *man is superior to the irrational animals*, or *whites and blacks are alike men*, that idea does not bring before me any man in particular. It leaves out of account all the individual characteristics which distinguish one man from another ; in the language of philosophy it *abstracts* from them.

This is proved by the fact that while remaining absolutely the same and without need of any modification whatsoever, it can be applied to the most dissimilar individuals ; Sancho Panza is just as much a man as Don Quixote. Moreover, when we cast our mind over the different sciences, that is to say, the different systems of ideas by which we know reality, we find that none of them is concerned with the individual as such. Chemistry, for instance, only studies in chlorine or nitrogen what is common to all the individual molecules of chlorine or nitrogen. And this must necessarily be the case. The individual as such explains nothing (for, since it represents only

itself, it obviously cannot account for anything else).[1]
Again, we have only to take any idea whatsoever and
fix our attention on what it presents to us, comparing
it with the images which form and dissolve around it,
to perceive at once the abstract nature of the idea.
In the transition from the image to the idea whatever
is individual evaporates, so to speak, slips between
our fingers, and vanishes. Take, for example, the
idea of *weapon* which I employ when I state that
man is the only animal obliged to manufacture its weapons.
As I pronounced the word *weapons*, I was no doubt
conscious of a halo, so to speak, of fluctuating images
surrounding the idea thus expressed, to any of which
I can at pleasure give a more definite shape, a *javelin*
very shadowy no doubt, a *flint axe*, a *cross-bow*, a
gun. . . . But of the individual characteristics of the
particular javelin, axe, bow, or gun as they appear
in my imagination with their distinctive form, colour,
and dimensions, nothing whatever remains in my idea
of weapon. Everything of the sort has disappeared.
Though what I apprehend by the idea is certainly
some thing, that some thing is of an entirely different
order (immaterial), it is simply a certain determination
of being, a certain nature, *an instrument of attack or
defence* ; and that is devoid of any individual character.

That is to say, objects as presented to us *by our
sensations and images* are presented in a state which is
individual, or in technical language *singular*. On the
contrary, objects as presented to us *by our ideas*, by
the internal likenesses which enable us to reason about
them, are presented in a state which is non-individual,
abstract, or in technical language *universal*.

[1] *Cf.* T. Richard, *op. cit.*, p. 21.

We call *universal* that which is the same in a multitude of individuals, one in many, *unum in multis*.) We shall therefore hold as an established truth that—

> *Conclusion VII.*—Our sensations and images present to us directly or by themselves the individual, our ideas directly and by themselves the universal.

But the question at once arises : Since real objects are individual or singular, how can the knowledge we obtain by means of our ideas be true, since our ideas directly present only the universal ?

This problem, which will compel us to investigate carefully in what exactly consists the universality of that which our ideas present, is, not indeed in itself, but at any rate for us men, the first and most important of philosophic problems.[1] For it is concerned with the nature of the intellect itself and of our ideas, that is to say, with the instrument by which all our knowledge is obtained ; and the solution propounded by different philosophers dominates their entire system.

From this point of view, and taking no account of many differences of secondary importance, we may classify philosophers in three great schools :

(a) The *nominalist* school, for which universals have

---

[1] Does the *problem of universals* belong to logic, psychology, or metaphysics (criticism or epistemology) ? To all three, in fact, according as it is studied from three different standpoints. We may inquire what constitutes the nature of a universal (standpoint of the *formal cause*), or the manner in which a universal is formed in the mind (standpoint of the *efficient cause*), or the epistemological value of the universal (standpoint of the *final cause*).

no existence except as names or ideas with which nothing in reality corresponds ; for instance, *there is nothing in the reality of* human nature *which is equally present in Peter, Paul, and John.* This position amounts to sheer negation of the possibility of intellectual knowledge, and reduces science to a figment of the mind. The most typical representatives of this school are, in antiquity the sophists and the sceptics, in modern times the leading English philosophers, William of Occam in the fourteenth century, Hobbes and Locke in the seventeenth, Berkeley and Hume in the eighteenth, John Stuart Mill and Spencer in the nineteenth. It may be added that the majority of *modern* philosophers (that is to say, of those who ignore or oppose the scholastic tradition) are more or less deeply, and more or less consciously, imbued with nominalism.

(*b*) The *realist* school (" *absolute realism* ") for which the universal as such, the universal taken separately, as it exists in thought, constitutes the reality of things. This position reduces sense-knowledge to mere illusion. *That which is real is, for example, a* human nature *existing in itself and separately outside the mind, a* man in himself (Platonism), *or a* universal being *existing as such outside the mind and regarded as the sole and unique substance* (doctrine of Parmenides, Vedantism). The systems of certain modern philosophers (Spinoza, Hegel) approximate more or less closely to realism.[1]

(*c*) The school which is usually called that of

[1] It must be borne in mind that realism understood in this sense, far from being incompatible with idealism, is essentially an idealist doctrine. For realism of this type regards as the reality of things that which is distinctive of our ideas as such. Plato is thus at once the most typical representative both of idealism and absolute realism.

moderate realism. (Its doctrine, however, is in the most strict sense original, and keeps the just mean between realism and nominalism, not by watering down or modifying absolute realism, but by a view of things which transcends the opposing errors.) This school, distinguishing between the thing itself and its mode of existence, the condition in which it is presented, teaches that a thing exists in the mind as a universal, in reality as an individual. Therefore that which we apprehend by our ideas as a universal does indeed really exist, but only in the objects themselves and therefore individuated—not as a universal. For example, *the* human nature *found alike in Peter, Paul, and John really exists, but it has no existence outside the mind, except in these individual subjects and as identical with them ; it has no separate existence, does not exist in itself.* This moderate realism is the doctrine of Aristotle and St. Thomas.

Philosophy of Aristotle and St. Thomas (Moderate Realism)

That which our ideas present to us as a universal does not exist outside the mind as a universal.	That which our ideas present to us as a universal exists outside the mind individuated.

Nominalism	*Realism*
That which our ideas present to us as a universal has no real existence whatsoever.	That which our ideas present to us as a universal really exists as a universal.

It is impossible to over-emphasise the importance of the problem of universals. It is for want of attention to it that so many philosophers and scientists of modern times cling to the naive belief that science must be a copy pure and simple, a tracing of the individual reality; serve up the stock arguments of ignorance against abstraction, the essential precondition of all human knowledge; and when treating of the principles of the sciences, especially of mathematics, spin elaborate theories, devoid of solid foundation, whose sole result is to render knowledge totally impossible.

III

THE PHILOSOPHY OF MATHEMATICS
THE PHILOSOPHY OF NATURE

THE distinctive object of theoretical philosophy is the being of things. The things which are immediately observed are corporeal things, bodies. But the term *body* may be taken in two distinct senses. It may mean a *mathematical* body, or a *natural* or physical body. A mathematical body is simply that which possesses three-dimensional extension, breadth, length, and height. A natural or physical body is that which is perceived by the senses as possessing certain active and passive properties.

THE PHILOSOPHY OF MATHEMATICS

If the *philosophy of mathematics* studies the being of bodies in the first sense of the term *body*, it is obvious that the first problem it must consider is in what does the primary object of mathematics consist ; in other words, what is the nature of quantity, extension, and number ? [1]

[1] Questions relating to the philosophy of mathematics are usually treated in natural philosophy or in metaphysics. We believe, however, that if classification is to be scientific, we are obliged to maintain in what is now known as philosophy (scientific knowledge of things by their first causes) the fundamental division of the sciences (the whole group of which constituted for the ancients theoretical philosophy) into three parts : *physica*, *mathematica*, *metaphysica*, corresponding to

The enormous progress made by modern mathematics has rendered more indispensable than ever before the philosophic study of the first principles of the mathematical sciences, which alone can provide a rational account of the true nature of mathematical abstraction and the mental objects which it considers, the properties and mutual relationships of the *continuous* and the *discontinuous*, the real meaning of *surds* and *transfinite numbers*, the *infinitesimal*, *non-Euclidean space*, etc., and finally of the validity of mathematical transcripts of physical reality, and of such hypotheses, for example, as the theory of relativity.

THE PHILOSOPHY OF NATURE [1]

Since the *philosophy of sensible nature* studies the being of bodies in the second sense of the term *body*, it

the three grades of abstraction (see p. 152). *Cf.* Aristotle, *Metaph.*, vi, 1, 1026 a 18. τρεῖς ἂν εἶεν φιλοσοφίαι θεωρητικαί, μαθηματική, φυσική, θεολογική.

It is true, as we shall see later, that the philosophy of mathematics, for the very reason that it studies the essence of quantity and is thus at least *reductively* metaphysical, transcends the strict sphere of the mathematical sciences and is specifically distinct from them. This, however, does not alter the fact that it is concerned with the second degree of abstraction and must therefore be studied as a separate branch of philosophy.

[1] In the logical order of the sciences, the natural sciences which correspond to the first degree of abstraction (see p. 152) precede the mathematical sciences, which correspond to the second, so that in accordance with this order we should be obliged to divide theoretical philosophy into (i) The *philosophy of nature* (corresponding to the first degree of abstraction), (ii) The *philosophy of mathematics* (corresponding to the second degree), (iii) *metaphysics* (corresponding to the third degree).

Nevertheless the philosophy of mathematics should precede natura philosophy for two reasons.

On the one hand, truths of the mathematical order are easier to

must deal with a large number of problems. We can, however, pick out the most important of these for mention here.

The most universal and obvious characteristic of the corporeal world, which is involved in every physical event, is change. Philosophers, in whose vocabulary change of every description is termed *motion*, must therefore inquire what motion is.

It is at once obvious that if motion exists, something must be moved, namely, bodies. Further, certain changes seem to affect the very substance of bodies ; as, for instance, when the chemical combination of hydrogen and oxygen produces a new body, water. How is this possible? We are compelled to ask what *corporeal substance* is.

(*a*) The *mechanists*—whether in their doctrine of the human soul they are materialists (Democritus, Epicurus, Lucretius, among the ancients, Hobbes in the seventeenth century, etc.) or spiritualists like

---

apprehend than truths of the natural order, which presuppose experience. For this reason children should be taught the elements of mathematics before the natural sciences, the study of which requires a more advanced age. (*Cf.* Aristotle, *Nic. Eth.*, vi ; St. Thomas, *Sup. Boet. de Trin.*, q. 5, a. 1, *ad* 3.)

We should therefore follow the same order in philosophy and lead the mind up to the study of natural philosophy by the study of the philosophy of mathematics.

On the other hand, and this is the more important consideration, natural philosophy with the last and highest of its sub-divisions, namely psychology, touches the frontier of metaphysics. It would be a breach of continuity to insert the philosophy of mathematics between natural philosophy and metaphysics.

In the seventeenth century Sylvester Maurus maintained—and in so doing was faithful to the Aristotelian tradition—that the natural order of study is as follows : (i) *logic*, (ii) *mathematics*, (iii) *physics*, (iv) *metaphysics*. (*Quaest. philos.*, i, q. vii.)

Descartes—reduce corporeal substance to *matter*, which in turn they confuse with quantity or geometrical extension. They can therefore admit no essential or specific difference among bodies, which are all modifications of one single substance. Moreover, the physical universe is for them devoid of *quality* and *energy*, since space and local motion alone are real, and the union of matter and spirit in a being such as man becomes absolutely unintelligible.

(*b*) Another school (*dynamism*) tends on the contrary to get rid of matter as a constituent of bodies. It culminates in the system of Leibniz, who reduced corporeal substance to units of a spiritual character (*monads*) analogous to souls. For Leibniz extension, indeed sensible reality as a whole, is nothing more than an appearance or a symbol, and the corporeal world as such is absorbed in the spiritual. The dynamism of Boscovich (eighteenth century), who reduced corporeal substance to *points of force*, and the modern physical theory which claims to explain everything in the physical universe as manifestations of one sole reality, *energy* (of which, however, its exponents fail to give a philosophic definition), may be regarded as degradations and materialisations of Leibniz's doctrine.

(*c*) The Aristotelian philosophy recognises in corporeal substance two substantial principles : (i) *matter* (*first matter*, *materia prima*), which, however, in no way represents, as in the conception of the mechanists, the imaginable notion of extension, but the idea of matter (that of which something else is made) in its utmost purity—it is what Plato called a sort of non-entity, simply that *of which* things are made, which in itself is nothing actual, a principle wholly indeterminate, incapable of separate existence, but capable of existing in conjunction with something else (the form) ; (ii) an active principle, which is so to speak, the living idea or soul of the thing, and which determines the purely passive first matter, somewhat as the form imposed upon it by the sculptor determines the clay, constituting with it one single thing actually existent, one single corporeal substance, which owes to it both that it is this or that kind of thing, that is to say, its specific nature, and its existence, somewhat as the form imposed by the sculptor makes a statue what it is. On account of this analogy with the external form of a statue (its accidental form) Aristotle gave the name of *form* (*substantial form*), which must be understood in a sense altogether special and technical, to this internal principle of which we are speaking, which determines the very being of corporeal substance.

The Aristotelian doctrine, which regards a body as a compound of *matter* (ὕλη) and *form* (μορφή), is known as *hylomorphism*. It accepts the reality, on the one hand, of matter, the corporeal world, and extension,[1] on the other of physical qualities,[2] also a distinction of nature or essence between the bodies which we regard as belonging to different species. It reveals the presence, even in inanimate bodies and living things devoid of reason, of a substantial principle, immaterial in its nature, which, however, differs from spirits in

[1] Extension of *quantity* is not, as the mechanists hold, the *substance* of bodies, but their first *accident*.

[2] *Qualities* are also accidents of corporeal substance. (See below, pp. 217–232 (substance and accident).)

the strict sense, in its incapacity to exist apart from matter. And it renders intelligible the union in the human being of matter and a spiritual soul which is the form of the human body, but differs from the other substantial forms inasmuch as it can exist apart from matter.

Philosophy of Aristotle and St. Thomas (*Hylomorphism*)

Every corporeal substance is a compound of two substantial and complementary parts, one passive and in itself wholly indeterminate (*matter*), the other active and the principle of determination (*form*).

Mechanism	*Dynamism*
Corporeal substance is regarded as something simple, a matter itself identified with *geometrical extension*.	Corporeal substance is explained either as units belonging to the category of pure *forms* and spirits (Leibnizian monadism) or as a manifestation of force or energy.

We have now to consider a class of bodies which possess a peculiar interest for us, and seem to be superior to all the others. They are living bodies, from the lowliest micro-organism to the human organism. The property which distinguishes them from all other bodies is *self-movement*. On that account common sense recognises in them a *soul* or principle of life, irreducible to any combination of physico-chemical factors or elements. If this is indeed the case, we must inquire whether there are not different kinds of soul, whether vegetables and animals possess a soul, etc. On the other hand certain philosophers (known by the general appellation of mechanists) claim that science will one day explain all the phenomena of life by the forces of lifeless matter, that is to say, that the living organism is simply a very complicated physico-chemical machine. This involves a problem of the first importance. What is life? What are the first principles which constitute the living organism?

But of all living things which possess a body the highest is man. Man is as it were a world apart, for the study of which we are in a peculiarly favourable position, because we know him from within by what is called *self-consciousness*. His most distinctive characteristic is the possession of intelligence or *reason*. If, however, intelligence is indeed something wholly immaterial, it follows that the science which studies man, though a branch of natural philosophy which treats of moving or sensible being, is in a sense intermediate between this department of philosophy and metaphysics which treats of the wholly immaterial.[1]

If it is the possession of intelligence or reason which makes man man, the problems which relate to his intellectual activity must, it would seem, dominate the entire science of man.[2] And in fact the

[1] The science of man occupies therefore a singular position (due to the very nature of its object) astride two distinct sciences, natural philosophy and metaphysics. It is for this reason that all questions involving the intellect and the strictly spiritual portion of psychology display in the case of man such extreme complexity and are, so to speak, overshadowed by matter. It is not surprising, therefore, that when the Thomists wished to investigate these questions in their purity they studied not man but the angels. Hence the extreme importance of the treatise *De Angelis*, not for theology alone, but also for philosophy and metaphysics.

[2] Observe that *psychology* as understood by the moderns does not correspond exactly to the ancients' treatment of the soul. Aristotle's περὶ ψυχῆς, *De Anima*, studies not only the human soul, but also the soul in general as the principle of life, whether vegetative, sensitive, or intellectual. Such a treatise therefore belongs to what we now call *biology* as well as to psychology.

fundamental problem of *psychology* is that of *the origin of ideas* : how we are to explain the presence in us of the ideas which enable us to reason about things and which present things to us as universals.

At this point we have been brought back by a different approach to the problem of universals which we have lately considered. We then noted that what our ideas immediately present to us is something non-individual or universal. We have now to ask how this knowledge of the universal is acquired by our minds.

We saw above that things as they are known by the senses and the imagination are presented as individuals. It is this particular man that I see, with this particular appearance actually impressing itself on my retina and distinguishing him from the other man I see beside him. Sense-knowledge is thus knowledge of the individual alone. The object as object of sensation or the object reproduced by an image is the object apprehended in its individuality. Since, therefore, what we know immediately by our ideas is not individual, the reason must be that our ideas are in fact *extracted* by us from our sensations and images, but in such a fashion that there enters into them nothing whatsoever of the object as it exists *as an object of sensation or reproduced by an image* (that is to say, as we shall see later, as the object of a knowledge steeped in materiality). Arising from images, but of a higher order than the image, and apprehending nothing of the object as reproduced by the image, our ideas must necessarily be unable to give us any knowledge of the object in its individuality.

Moreover, we could not possibly derive our ideas from things, except by way of our senses, which are in immediate contact with things. And we have only to observe the mental development of a child to be convinced that all our knowledge begins with the senses. Therefore intellectual knowledge (knowledge by means of ideas) must undoubtedly be derived from sense-knowledge.

On the other hand, since everything apprehended by sensations and images is characterised by individuality, our ideas must be extracted from images in such a way that nothing of the image, as such, enters into the idea.

But how is this process of extraction conceivable? If nothing whatever of the object as it is reproduced by the image enters into the object as it is apprehended by the idea, it is obvious that the idea is not the result of any combination or distillation of sensations or images. We are therefore compelled to postulate an agent of a higher order, the νοῦς ποιητικός, as the Peripatetics termed it, the *intellectus agens*—a kind of intellectual light (we may perhaps compare it to X-rays) which, when applied to the object presented to us by the image, draws out of it for our understanding something already contained in it but hidden, which the image by itself could never reveal. The something thus extracted and liberated from that which constitutes the individuality of the object (because it is liberated from that which constitutes the materiality of sense-knowledge) is the *form* or *intelligible likeness* of the object, which is, so to speak, imprinted on the intellect to determine it to know, by making it produce within itself by a vital reaction the idea in which it apprehends the object as a universal ; for example, the idea of *man* or *living being*, of *Aryan* or *Semite*.

We must, however, remember that what our ideas present thus as a universal is in itself (abstracting from its existence either in things or in the mind) neither individual nor universal, being purely and simply that which the thing is.[1]

We must also bear in mind that, if our intellect does not directly know the individual as such, it knows it indirectly. For, at the very moment when it thinks of an object by means of an idea, it turns to the images from which the idea has been drawn, which present the thing as an individual. And by thus reflecting on the images it apprehends, though indirectly and in a manner wholly superficial and totally inexpressible, the individuality of the thing.

> *Conclusion VIII.*—Our ideas are extracted (*abstracted*) from the sensible datum by the activity of a special faculty (the *intellectus agens* or *active intellect*) which entirely transcends the sensible order and is, as it were, the light of our understanding.

Philosophers term *abstraction* the operation by which we thus extract our ideas from the store of images accumulated by sense experience, ideas which represent that which the thing is, abstracting from its individuality.

Here we may add that abstraction admits of lesser and greater degrees. For instance, though the idea

---

[1] I.e. the *nature, essence,* or *quiddity,* of the object. See pp. 201, 206.

of *horse* is, like every idea, abstract, when we think of *horse* we can at the same time see or imagine horses, and thus know in the sensible order what we know at the same time by means of our idea in the intelligible order. If, on the other hand, we think of *angel* or *spirit*, the sole function of the more or less vague images which accompany the thought is, as we have already observed, to assist the intellect to function. In their own order they have no value as knowledge, for they tell us nothing. We can neither see nor imagine an angel or a spirit; in this case, therefore, we cannot at the same time know by our senses the thing we know by our intellect.

It is important to bear in mind that the things with which philosophy is primarily concerned belong to this second category. They cannot be known either by the senses or the imagination, but solely by the intellect.

It is to this higher degree of abstraction that the study of philosophy owes its special difficulty. Beginners are often perplexed when they suddenly exchange the literary studies on which they have been engaged hitherto, studies in which the imagination was employed equally with the intellect, for an exercise wholly intellectual. But this difficulty will soon pass, if they will not try to represent by the imagination objects of pure thought which are entirely unimaginable, such, for instance, as *essence, substance, accident, potentiality*, and *act*; a chimerical attempt, which will only cause needless headaches and effectually prevent them from understanding anything of philosophy.

If abstraction is indeed such an operation as we have described, it follows in the first place that man is endowed with a spiritual soul, the first principle of this function (for its result, our ideas, is incommensurable with sensations and images and of a purely immaterial order) ; and on the other hand, that it is of the very nature of this spiritual soul to be united to a body (for our ideas cannot be formed except by means of sensations and images, which in turn necessarily suppose bodily organs). We thus perceive how the problem of abstraction, or the origin of ideas, is bound up with another fundamental problem of psychology, which concerns the very essence of man : in what does the *human being* consist ? Does man possess a spiritual soul, wholly different from that of the beasts ? And if so what is the relationship between this soul and the human body ?

On the problem of the origin of ideas philosophers may be divided roughly into three main groups : (*a*) The *sensualists*, who hold that ideas are derived from the senses, but reduce ideas to sensations. (*b*) The partisans of *innate ideas*,[1] who recognise the essential distinction between ideas and sensations or images, but deny that we extract our ideas from the sense datum. (*c*) The school of *Aristotle and St. Thomas*, which holds that our ideas differ essentially from sensations and images, but that they are extracted

[1] We may so term this second group in default of a more suitable title, but only if we considerably widen its meaning. For in this class of philosophers we must include not only those who teach that our ideas exist in our minds from birth in the same way as our soul exists (the doctrine of innate ideas in the strict sense), but those who hold that they are immediately implanted in us by God or are seen by us in God (Berkeley, Malebranche), or are the arbitrary product of our mind imposing its laws on things (Kant).

from them by the operation of the spiritual light in us (νοῦς ποιητικός, *intellectus agens*).

The principal representatives of sensualism are Locke (seventeenth century) and John Stuart Mill (nineteenth century) in England, and Condillac (eighteenth century) in France. The sensualists are, as a rule, also nominalists, but the converse does not hold, and many philosophers whom we class here among the defenders of innate ideas betray, in modern times at least, the influence of nominalism. In the second class (the defenders of innate ideas) we must reckon Plato among the ancients, Descartes (seventeenth century) and Leibniz (seventeenth to eighteenth century) among the moderns. Though their explanations differ, all these hold that our ideas are innate. Kant (end of eighteenth century) also belongs to this group, though for him what is innate is not our ideas, but the *categories*, rules, or forms in accordance with which our mind manufactures the objects of knowledge.

Philosophy of Aristotle and St. Thomas

Our ideas are derived from the senses (and therefore from things) but by the operation of a spiritual faculty, and are essentially different from sensations and images.

Our ideas are essentially different from sensations and images, but are *abstracted* from them by the operation of a spiritual faculty.

Sensualism

Our ideas are derived from the senses, which are sufficient to produce them, and do not differ essentially from images and sensations.

Doctrine of Innate Ideas

Ideas differ essentially from sensations and images and are not derived from the senses (nor therefore from things, with which our senses alone are in immediate contact).

The answers which philosophers have given to the problem of human nature correspond strictly with the position they adopt towards the problem of abstraction. The sensualists, at least so far as they are faithful to the logic of their doctrine (Condillac, for example, was not), deny either that the soul exists (*materialists*), or that we can in any case know its existence (*phenomenalists*). The defenders of innate ideas, on the other hand, tend to regard man as a pure spirit which happens to be joined to a body—how, they find it difficult to explain (*dualism* or *exaggerated spiritualism*).[1] Finally, the school of Aristotle and St. Thomas teaches that man is a composite of two substantial principles, each incomplete in itself and the complement of the other, one of which is a spiritual and immortal soul (*animism*).

Philosophy of Aristotle and St. Thomas (Animism)

Two principles each incomplete in itself, one of which (the rational soul) is spiritual, form together a single substance (the human composite).

Error of Defect	*Error of Excess*
The human soul does not exist (*materialism*) or is unknowable (*phenomenalism*).	Man is a spirit accidentally united to a body (*exaggerated spiritualism*) : the soul and the body are two substances each complete in itself (*dualism*).

We should remark further that the position adopted by philosophers towards the origin of ideas also determines their attitude to the general problem of the

[1] This tendency recurs even in Kant (especially in ethics), though he, like the phenomenalists, denies that reason can demonstrate the existence of the soul.

existence of things known by the senses (the sensible or corporeal world) and of things invisible and spiritual, accessible to reason alone.

Philosophy of Aristotle and St. Thomas
(also of common sense)

It is impossible without absurdity to doubt either the existence of corporeal objects (attested by the senses) or the existence of spiritual objects (proved by reason).

Systems more or less *Materialist*	*Systems more or less* *Idealist*
Nothing exists which is not perceptible by the senses and material (*absolute materialism*); or at least its existence is unknowable (*phenomenalist materialism* and *positivism*).	The world perceived by the senses has no real existence (*absolute idealism*); or at least its existence is unknowable and doubtful (*phenomenalist idealism*).

IV

CRITICISM (EPISTEMOLOGY)

IN studying *man* philosophy is dealing with an object which already by an entire portion of itself transcends the corporeal world, that is to say, the world of sensible nature. But it has the power and duty to go further, and since its distinctive object is the *being* of things, it must study that being no longer as corporeal, sensible, or moving (the subject-matter of the philosophy of sensible nature), but simply *as being* ; consequently it must study being under an aspect absolutely universal, and as it is present not only in visible things but also in things which possess no corporeal, sensible, or mobile being ; that is to say, in things which are purely spiritual. This is the object of that branch of philosophy which is philosophy or wisdom *par excellence*, and is known as the first philosophy or *metaphysics*.[1]

CRITICISM (EPISTEMOLOGY)

But before undertaking this study, the philosopher must secure against all possible attack or distortion the

---

[1] The name *metaphysics* originated in the fact that in the catalogue of Aristotle's works drawn up by Andronicus of Rhodes, the treatise dealing with the first philosophy (Περὶ τῆς πρώτης φιλοσοφίας, the title probably which Aristotle himself would have given to it) comes *after* the books which treat of *nature* (Μετὰ τὰ φυσικά). It would seem, however that chronologically Aristotle followed the same order in the actual composition of his works.

principles of this sovereign science, which are also the principles of all human knowledge. For it is the office of wisdom to defend its own principles and those of the other sciences.

It will therefore be necessary, before studying being in itself, as such, to study the relation of human thought to being. This is the object of a special department of metaphysics, known as *criticism*, because it has the function of judging knowledge itself. *Logic* shows how and in accordance with what rules reason attains truth and acquires knowledge ; this in turn pre-supposes the possibility of true knowledge (a possibility attested by common sense and evident by the light of nature). Criticism submits this presupposition to scientific treatment, showing in what the truth of knowledge consists, and establishing by a reflex argument that true, certain, and scientific knowledge is undoubtedly attainable.[1]

What is the truth of knowledge, and is it possible to refute those who question the veracity of our organs of knowledge, particularly of the intellect or reason ? This clearly is the double question which arises at the outset. The answer, however, is sufficiently plain.

As to the first question, there is no difficulty in under-standing what is meant by the notion of *truth*. What is a true or truthful word ? A word which expresses, as it really is, the speaker's thought ; a word in

---

[1] By thus distinguishing criticism (epistemology) from logic, and making it the first part, special introduction, or if you prefer, apologetic introduction, to metaphysics, we are faithful to the arrangement and divisions of Aristotle himself, who discusses criticism briefly (*Metaph.*, iv) before studying the great problems of being as such.

conformity with that thought. What, then, is a true thought? A thought which represents, as it really is, the thing to which it refers ; a thought in conformity with that thing. We therefore conclude that *truth in the mind* consists in its *conformity with the thing*.

It is impossible to define truth otherwise without lying to ourselves, without falsifying the notion of truth of which in practice we make use, in the living exercise of our intelligence, each time that we think.

We may further remark that a thought false in all its constituents is an impossibility for, being in conformity with nothing whatsoever, it would be the zero of thought. If, for instance, I affirm that *stones have a soul*, this is undoubtedly a complete error. But it is true that stones exist, true also that certain beings have a soul ; that is to say, all the constituents which compose this false thought are not false. Therefore error itself presupposes truth.[1]

We may also observe that if man were really and seriously to doubt the veracity of his organs of knowledge he simply could not live. Since every action or abstention from action is an act of trust in that veracity, action and inaction would alike become impossible. A man therefore who attempted to carry out in his life the thought *truth is impossible for me* would inevitably lose his reason. Nietzsche, who was a great poet but regarded belief in truth as the ultimate bondage from which the world should be delivered, made the experiment to his cost.

---

[1] *Cf. Sum. Theol.*, ii–ii, q. 172, a. 6 : *Sicut se habet bonum in rebus, ita verum in cognitione. Impossibile est autem inveniri aliquid in rebus, quod totaliter bono privetur : unde etiam impossibile est esse aliquam cognitionem quae totaliter sit falsa absque admixtione alicujus veritatis.*

As for the *sceptics*, who doubt, at least theoretically and in words, the reliability of our organs of knowledge, especially of the intellect or reason, it would obviously be waste of breath to attempt to demonstrate its reliability to them. For every demonstration rests on some previously admitted certainty, and it is their very profession to admit of none. To defend human knowledge against their attack it is sufficient (i) to show in what that knowledge consists and how it is attained ; (ii) to refute the arguments they adduce ; (iii) to make a *reductio ad absurdum*. When they say that they do not know whether any proposition is true, either they know that this proposition at any rate is true, in which case they obviously contradict themselves, or they do not know whether it is true, in which case they are either saying nothing whatever, or do not know what they say. The sole philosophy open to those who doubt the possibility of truth is absolute silence—even mental. That is to say, as Aristotle points out, such men must make themselves vegetables. No doubt reason often errs, especially in the highest matters, and, as Cicero said long ago, there is no nonsense in the world which has not found some philosopher to maintain it, so difficult is it to attain truth. But it is the error of cowards to mistake a difficulty for an impossibility.

Conclusion IX.—The truth of knowledge consists in the conformity of the mind with the thing. It is absurd to doubt the reliability of our organs of knowledge.

On this question of the reliability of our organs of

knowledge philosophers may again be divided—roughly—into three groups :

(*a*) The *sceptics*, who, impressed by the enormous number of errors put forward by men, and especially by philosophers, doubt the trustworthiness of reason, and affirm that truth is impossible of attainment. The principal representatives of scepticism are, among the ancients, Pyrrho (360–270), the neo-Academics (Arcesilas 315–241 ; Carneades, 214–129) and the later Greek sceptics (Aenesidemus, first century A.D., and Sextus Empiricus, end of the second century); in modern times Montaigne and Sanchez in the sixteenth century, and pre-eminently David Hume in the eighteenth.

The philosophers called *anti-intellectualists*, because they despair of intellect and reason, and look for truth to the will, to instinct, feeling, or action (Rousseau, Fichte, Schopenhauer, Bergson, William James, the modernist and pragmatist school), must be classified with the sceptics, because, although they do not, like the sceptics strictly so called, declare truth unattainable, they maintain that it is unattainable by the organ whose distinctive nature it is to discover truth, and because by rejecting the intellect and reason they effectually deprive man of his sole normal means of attaining it.

(*b*) The *rationalists*, on the contrary, are of opinion that truth is easy to attain, and therefore undertake to bring all things within the compass of reason, a human reason which has no need to submit humbly and patiently to the discipline, whether of reality itself, a teacher, or God. In the first case they tend to *subjectivism*, which takes as its criterion of truth the knowing subject, not the object to be known ; a position which is the dissolution of knowledge. In the second they tend to *individualism*, which calls upon each philosopher to work out a philosophy entirely his own, and create an original and novel view of the universe (*Weltanschauung*). In the third, they tend to *naturalism*, which claims to attain to a perfect wisdom by the unassisted powers of nature, and rejects all divine teaching.[1]

The father of modern rationalism was *Descartes* (seventeenth century), to whom Malebranche, Spinoza, and Leibniz traced more or less directly their philosophic pedigree. But its first principles and true spirit were revealed by *Kant* (end of eighteenth century), who completed the Cartesian revolution ; his pantheistic successors, Fichte, Schelling, and Hegel, deified the human subject of knowledge. Through *Kant*, and the *subjectivist* philosophy which traces its origin to him, rationalism, as before in the era of the sophists, has joined hands with its opposite (scepticism), and become absorbed in the anti-intellectualism of the *modernists* (end of the nineteenth and beginning of the twentieth century).

(*c*) The school of *Aristotle and St. Thomas* teaches that truth is neither impossible nor easy, but difficult for man to attain.

It is thus radically opposed alike to scepticism and to rationalism. It sees in the multitude of errors put

---

[1] Naturalism rejects divine teaching in these two different ways : (1) It denies God the right to teach men truths in themselves inaccessible to the unassisted reason (*supernatural mysteries*). (2) It also denies him the right to teach men by revelation truths in themselves accessible to unassisted reason (truths of the natural order, *philosophic truths*—for example, the immortality of the human soul) which reason can indeed discover by its unaided powers, but always with the risk of mingling error with truth, whereas revelation brings them within the reach of all, easily and without any admixture of error.

forward by men and particularly by philosophers a sign indeed of the weakness of the human understanding, but a reason to prize the intellect the more dearly and to embrace truth the more ardently, and an instrument for the advancement of knowledge by the refutations and explanations which these errors call forth. And, on the other hand, it recognises that reason is our sole natural means of attaining truth, but only when formed and disciplined, in the first place and pre-eminently by reality itself (for our mind is not the measure of things, but things the measure of our mind), secondly by teachers (for science is a collective, not an individual, achievement, and can be built up only by a continuous living tradition), and finally by God, if he should please to instruct mankind and bestow upon philosophers the negative rule of faith and theology.[1]

Philosophy of Aristotle and St. Thomas
(Moderate Intellectualism)

That which really is the cause of truth in the mind. Reason is capable of attaining with complete certainty the most sublime truths of the natural order, but with difficulty and only when duly disciplined.

Error by Defect	*Error by Excess*
Reason is incapable of attaining truth, which either is wholly inaccessible to man (*scepticism*) or must be sought otherwise than by the intellect (*anti-intellectualism*).	Reason attains truth in every sphere easily and without any need of submitting to any external discipline (*rationalism*).

Synthesis of these Two Errors

The mind of man makes the truth of that which he knows (namely, phenomena), and that which really is, the thing in itself, is unknowable by reason (*criticism* or *Kantian agnosticism*).

[1] See above, p. 124.

Another question, among those with which criticism is concerned, demands consideration here. The intellect or reason being the instrument of philosophy, what is the formal object of the intellect, to which intellectual knowledge relates directly and in itself?

To answer this question it is sufficient to ask oneself whether there does not exist an object which is always present to the mind when the intellect functions? Such an object does exist. Whatever I know by my intellect, there is always some being or mode of being present to my mind. There is, however, nothing else except being which is always present in this way. If, for example, I think of a *quality*, a *magnitude*, or a *substance*, in all these cases alike I think of some being or mode of being ; but there is nothing except being which is common to these three objects of thought, and therefore present in all three alike. We therefore conclude that *being* is the formal object of intellect, that is to say, the object which it apprehends primarily and in itself (*per se primo*) and in function of which it apprehends everything else.

To know the cause of a thing, its purpose, origin, properties, and relations with other things, is in these various ways to know what it is, to apprehend its being under those different aspects. To use the understanding without the notion of being arising is an impossibility.

The intellect, moreover, is able to apprehend the being of bodies in their sensible appearances (*pheno-mena*). It is thus, for example, that in physiology it studies the properties of living organisms in reference to causes which themselves belong to the sensible order. Of this nature are the sciences of secondary causes or the sciences of phenomena. But the intellect can also apprehend the being of things in their first principles. This is the function of philosophy as a whole, which in turn is subdivided into *natural philosophy* and *metaphysics*, according as the being apprehended in its first principles by the intellect is the being of bodies as such or being simply as being.

Psychology indeed deals with this question of the formal object of the intellect. But the distinctive function of criticism is to make clear that the being with which we are here concerned is indeed the actual being of things, which exists in them *independently* of the knowing mind. To maintain on the contrary that the object of our intellect is not the being of things but the *idea* of being which it forms in itself, or more generally that we apprehend immediately only our ideas,[1] is to deliver oneself bound hand and foot to scepticism. For if that were the case, it would be impossible for our mind under any circumstances to conform itself to that which really is, and truth would therefore be unattainable. Moreover, the intellect would stand convicted of falsehood, for what the intellect professes to know is what things are, not what its ideas are. In reality ideas, as the consciousness of every man witnesses immediately, are our *instruments* of knowledge. If, therefore, knowledge did not apprehend the things themselves, knowing would be an operation or activity without end or object, which is absurd. For to form an idea or judgment is to know, just as to make use of a knife is to cut. And, just as it is impossible to cut without cutting something

[1] The doctrine of Descartes and after him of all subjective philosophy.

—the end or object of the act of cutting, which is not the knife, but the thing cut by it—so it is impossible to know without knowing something—the end or object of the act of knowing, which is not the idea, but the thing known by it.[1]

> *Conclusion X.*—The formal object of the intellect is being. What it apprehends of its very nature is what things are independently of us.

From the two truths just enunciated, *the intellect is a truthful faculty*, and *being is the necessary and immediate object of the intellect*, there arises as a corollary a fundamental truth.

By *intelligible* we mean *knowable by the intellect*. But to affirm that being is the necessary and immediate object of the intellect, and that the intellect attains true knowledge, amounts to saying that being, as such, is an object of which the intellect possesses true knowledge ; that is to say, that it is intelligible. And to say that being as such is intelligible is to say that intelligibility accompanies being, so that everything is intelligible in exact proportion to its being. We therefore conclude—

> *Conclusion XI.*—Being as such is intelligible. Everything is intelligible in exact proportion to its being.

[1] Intellectual knowledge comes into existence by means of ideas. But ideas are simply that by means of which (*id quo*), not that which (*id quod*) we know directly, a pure *medium* of knowledge, not (unless reflexively) an object or *term* known. This is why we say that the being of things is the *immediate* object of our intellectual knowledge (by *immediate* we mean *known without the intermediary of another* term *or* object *previously known*).

It must be borne in mind that when we affirm that everything is intelligible in exact proportion to its being we mean intelligible *in itself*, to intellect, not intelligible to us, to our intellect. If, indeed, as a result of the inferiority of human nature, our intellect is disproportioned to a being which exceeds it because it is superior to man, that being, though in itself more intelligible, will be less intelligible to us. This, however, is the case with all wholly spiritual natures, and pre-eminently of God. In himself he is the most intelligible of beings, but his intellect alone is proportionate to this supreme intelligibility.

V

ONTOLOGY : ESSENCE

HAVING in criticism examined and defended the principles of knowledge in general, whether scientific or philosophic, we can proceed to the study of metaphysics in the strict sense, that is to say, the science of being *qua* being. This is the very heart of philosophy. We have now to consider being as such, and the great truths it contains in itself; to inquire how it enters into all things without being exhausted by any; to study its inseparable properties, unity, truth, and goodness, to which we may add beauty; and finally to treat of it in its activity, and attempt to penetrate the nature and modes of causation.

We must also examine how throughout the entire created universe being is divided, whether we consider the constitution of all created being (division of being into *potentiality* and *act*, *essence* and *existence*) or the different kinds of created beings (division of being into *substance* and *accident*). We shall then realise that the concepts elucidated by *ontology* are the key to everything else. Certain among them are indeed so indispensable that we must consider them here, for indeed at every turn we are obliged to invoke the primary concepts of *essence*, of *substance* and *accident*, of *potentiality* and *act*. Though it is obviously impossible in a mere introduction to give an analysis and complete defence of these concepts, we shall try to establish them with all due care, employing, it is true, examples rather than developed arguments, and simplifying matters considerably, but following nevertheless the order demanded by a strictly scientific study.

Although the notion of *being*, since it is the first and best known of all, is evidently too clear in itself to admit of definition in the strict sense, the first task incumbent on a man who wishes to think seriously is to clarify this notion in his mind, and with that object to discover the primary conceptions into which it is divided.[1] We shall therefore begin by asking the following question : What are the objects of thought which inevitably and from the very outset impose themselves upon the intellect when it considers being as such, or to put it in another way, since being is the primary object of intellect, what are absolutely the first data of the intellect ? [2]

We shall see that this one fundamental question admits of three answers according as we adopt the

[1] *Cf.* Aristotle, *Metaph.*, v.

[2] The notions explained in pp. 191 *sqq.* present some difficulty to beginners on account of their extremely abstract character. It is, however, impossible to omit them, for they are literally of primary importance. And in particular we are convinced of the urgent necessity to define with the utmost care, from the very outset, the fundamental concept of *essence*. Materials for the study of this concept are scattered in different places, but is it not because we have forgotten to collect them that the term *essence*, when we meet it on the threshold of metaphysics, arouses to-day such suspicion, and, even if it forces itself on our acceptance, leaves such vagueness in the mind ?

The student must therefore devote particular attention to the study of the notions here explained, without, however, attempting to comprehend them perfectly. For the moment it will be sufficient to make his first acquaintance with them. Later when he meets them again in ontology, after he has become more familiar with philosophy, they will seem much easier.

standpoint of *intelligibility*, of *existence*, or of *action*. The consideration of the first of these standpoints will lead us to determine what is meant by *essence*, of the second to determine what is meant by *substance* (as opposed to *accident*), of the third to determine what is meant by *act* (as opposed to *potentiality*).

ESSENCE

We shall first consider being from the standpoint of intelligibility ; that is to say, we shall consider being so far as it is adapted to enter the mind, or is capable of being apprehended by the intellect. This is the most universal standpoint we can adopt, for we have seen that being as such is intelligible and hence that intelligibility is co-extensive with that which is or can be. To *the primary datum of the intellect* from this point of view we shall give the name of *essence*.

(*a*) To consider being from the standpoint of intelligibility or as it is capable of being apprehended by the intellect is in the first place to consider it so far as it can be simply presented to the mind without affirmation or negation—in so far as it can be the object of simple apprehension, as we shall term it later. *Triangle*, *polygon*, *seated*, *this man*, are so many objects simply presented to the mind without being affirmed or denied.

From this point of view the primary datum of the intellect is quite simply that which is placed at the outset before our mind when we form the conception of anything, or conceive the idea of it. Since we have agreed to use the term *essence* in this sense, we conclude that an essence is that which in any object of thought whatsoever is immediately and primarily (*per se primo*) presented to the intellect : *id quod in aliqua re per se primo intelligitur*.

Every idea whatsoever, unless it be, like the idea of *a square circle*, a pseudo-idea involving a contradiction, brings immediately before the mind something. The something thus immediately presented to the mind is an essence or a *nature*. When I think of *man*, *humanity*, *animal*, *goodness*, *white*, *whiteness*, *seated*, *triangle*, etc., each of the objects thus immediately presented to my mind, each of these intelligible units is by definition an *essence* in the wide sense of the word.[1]

An essence therefore is simply an object of thought as such. Every essence, however, possesses its intelligible constitution which distinguishes it from others and involves certain attributes.

Here, however, an important observation must be made. If I consider *the triangle* with its properties, *man*, *humanity*, etc., they remain exactly what they are as objects of thought, whether I suppose them actually to exist or not. The fact of existence does not in any way affect essences as such. To conceive them I

[1] We have already seen that the individual as such is not directly apprehended by our intellect. When indirectly, by a reflection on the images (see above, p. 172), we form an individual concept, the object presented to our mind by this concept, *Peter*, *this man*, *this tree*, is also, so far as it is an object of thought, an essence in the wide sense of the term. That is to say, the concept of essence in the wide sense must be extended even to individual objects of thought. As for those *conceptual beings* (*blindness*, for example, or *nothingness*) which present nothing that really exists, the name *essence* is inapplicable to them for the reason that a privation as such has obviously no essence. (See St. Thomas, *De Ente et Essentia*, i.) Nevertheless, from our present standpoint, we may call them improperly *essences*, in the wide sense.

abstract from the fact that they do or do not actually exist.

We thus perceive that *being* in the sense of *existence* and *being* in the sense of *essence* belong to two distinct categories.[1] The term *being* has two wholly different meanings. For example, in the quotation " to be or not to be, that is the question," *being* means *existence*, but on the contrary in the phrase *a living being* it means *essence*. In the first case the term *being* signifies the *act* of being, the act, if I may so put it, which posits a thing outside nonentity, and outside its causes (*extra nihil, extra causas*) ; and in the second case it signifies *that* which is or may be, that which corresponds to some existence actual or possible. We may therefore say that *being* is divided into *essence* and *existence*.

BEING (*ens*) (*entitas*) { *that* which is : *essence* in the wide sense (*essentia*)
act of being : *existence* (*existentia*)

The relationship which obtains between these two terms is a problem which we shall study later ; it is, beyond question, not simply with reference to ourselves, like the problem of universals, but in itself the fundamental problem of philosophy : are essence and existence really distinct in all things except God ?

Actual existence, the fact of existing actually, is not

[1] Observe that in existence itself we may distinguish two things : existence as the fact of existing (*existere in actu exercito*) and existence as an object of thought (*existentia ut quod quid est*). Regarded from the latter point of view existence itself assumes the objective status of every object of thought and confronts the intellect as a particular essence or *quiddity*. *Esse dupliciter sumi potest, scilicet in actu exercito ipsius existentiae, et per modum quidditatis ; et ut exercet existentiam, addit supra seipsum ut quod quid est ; et consequenter ut objectum intellectus est abstractius (quam ut objectum voluntatis) : quia est objectum voluntatis secundum quod stat in actu exercito existentiae, intellectus autem secundum quod rationem habet quidditatis cujusdam in seipso.* Cajetan, *in I*, q. 82, a. 3.

included in the object of any of our ideas as such. Our intellect can ascribe actual existence to a particular object of thought only by basing itself directly or indirectly by means of ratiocination on the witness of our senses (or reflexively of our consciousness). Thus it immediately judges *sensible objects exist, I exist*, and demonstrates the existence of God by arguing, for example, from the observed fact of motion. It cannot by itself alone attain the actual existence of the objects of its thought.

Those essences, on the other hand (such as *triangle, even numbers, humanity*), which of their nature connote only a *possible* existence (for which reason they are also called *possibles*), are data furnished immediately by our intellect and ideas.

We must now examine more closely this notion of essence, or being understood as *that* which is or can be. We have just defined an essence : that which in any object of thought whatsoever is immediately and primarily presented to the intellect : *id quod in aliqua re per se primo intelligitur*. Let us see whether this extremely wide concept (for it is applicable to any object of thought) may not be subdivided and qualified in such a way that the same definition taken in a more restricted sense shall henceforward be applicable, in each particular instance, only to a particular object of thought.

(*b*) The mere presentation to the mind of an object of thought (*man, white*) is but the beginning of intellectual knowledge, which is perfect only in the judgment by which the mind affirms or denies this object of thought in reference to another (*Peter is a man, this flower is white*). If then we would consider being from the standpoint of intelligibility, to discover what is from this point of view the absolutely primary datum of the intellect, we must consider objects of thought so far as they can be apprehended by the intellect when it judges, for example when it affirms that *Peter is a man*. From this point of view which, among the various objects of thought which can be realised in a given subject, is that which the intellect apprehends immediately and before everything else? We shall call it *essence* in the strict sense of the term.

Consider any object of thought, for example, *Peter, Paul, this dog, this bird*: *Peter* is tall, *Paul* is laughing and moving, *this dog* is barking, *this bird* is flying. Each of these is a particular whole, individual, concrete, and independent, completely equipped for existence and action.

It is individual subjects of this kind that our mind apprehends before anything else (from the standpoint of existence) when we think of that which is. When applied to objects of this kind the expression *that which is* acquires a more definite and special force. It no longer simply means that which corresponds to some actual or possible existence, but *that which* fulfils in the strictest sense and before everything else the act of being. These objects are all, though in very diverse respects, actors in the drama of the universe.

When, however, we adopt the standpoint of intelligibility, our mind does not among the different objects of thought which things can present apprehend in the first place these individual subjects as such. On the contrary the individual, as we have seen above, escapes the direct grasp of the intellect. What I know of *Peter* is *what* I know he is—for example, a

195

man. It is such objects of thought as *man* or *humanity* which it perceives in *Peter,* or such as *white* or *whiteness* which it perceives in *this flower,* it is *what* a thing is that, from this point of view, our mind primarily apprehends, and it is therefore in this direction that we must look for the absolutely first datum of the intellect in relation to intelligibility (essence in the strict sense).

The concept of essence in the wide sense has thus been subdivided into two. There is in the first place that which in the strict sense is, *that which.* And in the second place what a thing is, *what.*

BEING $\begin{cases} \textit{that} \text{ which is : } \textit{essence} & \begin{cases} \textit{what} \\ \textit{that which} \end{cases} \\ \quad \text{in the wide sense} \\ \\ \textit{act} \text{ of being : } \textit{existence} \end{cases}$

That which is in the strict sense we shall entitle the *primary subject of existence and action.* It is what philosophers also term *suppositum* and *person.* For the moment we may neglect it, for, as we shall see, it does not concern our present inquiry.

Let us, on the contrary, consider *what* a thing is. In the notion of what a thing is there are further distinctions and exclusions to be made, to determine more precisely what is actually the absolutely primary datum of the intellect from the standpoint of intelligibility and therefore deserves to be entitled *essence* in the strict sense of the term ; what, for example, is the essence of Peter. *Peter is seated. Peter is capable of laughter. Peter is a man.* Is what is here predicated of Peter—*seated, capable of laughter, man*—in each of these three cases, or in one alone, the being which the intellect apprehends in Peter immediately and primarily from the standpoint of intelligibility ? We said above that every object of thought is, as such, an essence (*essence* in the wide sense). Now we are studying what Peter is, and inquiring what is the object of thought which constitutes the essence of Peter (*essence* in the strict sense).

The following are the *characteristics* of the object of thought thus defined, that is, of the being primarily apprehended by the intellect when it considers *what* a thing is.

It is at once plain that the being to which the intellect is directed in the first place when it thinks what a thing is, is a being which the intellect cannot conceive that thing lacking or deprived of.

It is in fact in terms of that being that the intellect immediately conceives, apprehends, grasps, sets before itself and names the object in question. To deprive the thing of that being, or to alter its constitution in any way, would be to set before the intellect, by definition, a different thing.

It is thus a being which that thing so far as it exists cannot lack or be deprived of (otherwise the intellect would not be truthful). For example, *Peter*, so far as he exists, cannot be other than a *man* ; on the other hand, he can be *not seated*.

The being in question is therefore a being which the thing considered by the intellect is *necessarily and immutably*.

Moreover, it is obviously the being which in the thing possesses primary importance for the intellect, since it is that to which the intellect is first directed. It is thus the being which before anything else [1] the

---

[1] It is plain that the word *before* denotes in this connection a priority of nature, not of time.

object is, and is, so to speak, the ground of what the object is in other respects. It is the *first* being of the thing. Peter, for example, is a *man* before he is *capable of laughter* or *mortal*.

We conclude that the being to which the intellect is in the first place directed when it thinks what a thing is, is its *necessary* and *first* being, or, in short, the being which constitutes the thing, what it necessarily and primarily is.

This is the first characteristic of what we have agreed to call *essence* in the strict sense.

There is a second. It was the standpoint of intelligibility, it will be remembered, which we adopted when we undertook this study of essence. Peter is a *man* (*rational animal*) before being *mortal*. That is, *man* includes *animal*, and in the notion of *animal* the intellect finds the necessary characteristic, *mortal*. The characteristics *mortal* and *capable of laughter*— necessarily possessed by Peter—have in him a principle and ground, which by its very notion, or by what it is, or its own intelligibility, compels the intellect to posit these characteristics, and this principle or ground is one of the elements or aspects which constitute the being *man*. It is from the standpoint of intelligibility that Peter is a *man* before being *mortal* or *capable of laughter*.

Thus if the being *man* is, as we have said, first, it is in the order of intelligibility that it is first. In other words, it is in Peter the first principle of intelligibility.[1] However long our formula, we must say, if we would express this truth exactly, that the being *man* is in

---

[1] *Non enim res intelligibilis est nisi per suam definitionem et essentiam.* St. Thomas, *De Ente et Essentia*, i.

virtue of its constituent elements or aspects the root of all the characteristics necessarily possessed by Peter [1] which have in Peter *a principle which by its very notion requires them.*

This, then, is the second characteristic of what we have agreed to call *essence* in the strict sense ; of the being to which the intellect is directed in the first place when it considers *what* things are. It is in the thing the *first principle of intelligibility.*

Our intellect apprehends this being which is the first principle of intelligibility in two ways, one imperfect, the other perfect.

If, for example, we know that an object is a *man,* without, however, being able to state what *man* is, we possess a confused knowledge of the being in question. Our intellect grasps that being, has truly apprehended it, and really perceives it, but, so to speak, after the fashion in which our eyes see an opaque object.

If, however, we know this same object and are able to define *what* it is (*an animal endowed with reason*) we now possess a distinct knowledge of the being in question.

Our intellect not only perceives it, but also perceives its principles or constituent aspects.

In the first instance the being in question is presented to us imperfectly, in the second perfectly, with the perfection demanded by science, so that we can employ it as a first principle of intelligibility. (For example, from the knowledge that this thing is *endowed with reason* I can deduce that it is *capable of speaking, laughing, worshipping God,* etc.) But in both instances it is obviously the same being which is presented to

[1] These characteristics are termed *properties.*

us. Therefore, though I do not yet know or even can never know this particular being distinctly as a *rational animal*, in itself it will be none the less (though in this case I do not know how) in virtue of its constituent elements the root of all the characteristics which possess in Peter a principle requiring them by its very notion ; it will be none the less in itself the primary being of the thing as the first principle of its intelligibility.

We now know what are the characteristics of essence in the strict sense and are in a position to define it as follows : Essence is the necessary and primary being of a thing as the first principle of intelligibility, or, in other words, what a thing necessarily and primarily is as intelligible, in short, the primary intelligible being of a thing : *id quod per se primo intelligitur in aliqua re.*[1]

BEING {
  that which is : {
    essence in the wide sense {
      what a thing is primarily as intelligible } *essence* in the strict sense
      that which : the subject of action (*suppositum, person*)
    }
  }
  act of being : *existence*
}

---

[1] Essence considered as an attribute of the thing (for example, *man* when we say *Peter is a man*) is strictly what the thing is necessarily and primarily as intelligible. Essence considered separately and in the pure state (for example, when we speak of *humanity* or *the being man*, we cannot say *Peter is humanity* or *Peter is the being man*) is strictly that *in virtue of which* a thing is what it is necessarily and primarily as intelligible, or, to put it in another way, that in virtue of which it is constituted in a determinate degree of primarily intelligible being. If therefore we consider essence in the pure state, we must substitute in our synopses for the expression *what* the expression *that in virtue of which* :

BEING {
  that which is : {
    essence in the wide sense {
      that in virtue of which a thing is what it is primarily as intelligible } *essence* in the strict sense
      that which : the subject of action (*suppositum, person*)
    }
  }
  act of being : *existence*
}

Conclusion XII.—The essence of a thing is what that thing is necessarily and primarily as the first principle of its intelligibility.

This primary datum of the intellect is termed by philosophers not only the *essence* but also the *quiddity* and *nature*. It is what Aristotle and the schoolmen called the τό τι ἦν εἶναι, the *quod quid est*,[1] and which they defined as *id quod per se primo intelligitur in aliqua re*,[2] a definition with which we were already acquainted, but to which we have now attached a completely definite sense.

The definition, when used of essence in the wide sense, meant *what a particular* idea *first presents to the intellect*. When employed of essence in the strict sense, it means *what a particular* subject *primarily is for the intellect*.

Observe that every object of thought, every essence whatsoever (*essence* in the wide sense) is in fact the essence of something (*essence* in the strict sense) apprehended more or less completely (in some or other of its properties). When I think of *animal*, I apprehend the essence of *Peter* in one part of its properties. When I think of *man* I apprehend it as a whole. When I think of *Aryan*, *Breton*, or *Peter* I apprehend it as a whole with the addition of certain characteristics or attributes derived from the matter (see below, pp. 207–216). When I think of *a living body endowed with sensibility* I apprehend the entire essence of the subject

---

[1] The Latin equivalent of the Greek term is *quod quid erat esse*—as St. Thomas explains (*De Ente et Essentia*, i), *id est hoc per quod aliquid habet esse quid*, that which makes any object of thought this or that particular thing.

[2] Or stated more fully : *id quod primo in re concipitur, sine quo res esse non potest, estque fundamentum et causa ceterorum quae sunt in eadem re : ut animal rationale est hominis essentia*.

animal (and at the same time the essence of the subject *Peter* in one part of its properties). When I think of *white* or *prudence*, I perceive the essence of a particular quality. When I think of *goodness*, *unity*, *being*, I apprehend a certain created participation of the Divine Essence (or I apprehend, by analogy, if I think of *subsistent goodness*, etc., the Divine Essence itself).

Observe, further, that every subject capable of forming part of any proposition whatsoever [1] has an essence distinctively its own, whether it be an individual subject such as *Peter* (*substantia prima*, subject par excellence), an abstract and universal subject (*substantia secunda*) such as *animal*, an accident, for example, a particular colour or virtue, or a transcendental, for instance *the one*, *the good*, etc.

The primary intelligible being of a thing is called *essence* (*essentia*) because since the intellect is modelled on being, what a thing primarily is for the intellect must be that which is of primary importance in it from the standpoint of being itself; in fact, as we shall see later, it is by and in its *essence* that a thing possesses being or *existence* (*esse*).[2] It is called *quiddity* (*quidditas*) because it is that which the definition expresses and declares, which in turn answers the question *quid est hoc? What is this?* It is called *nature* (*natura*) because it is the first principle of the operations for the performance of which the thing has come into being (*nata*).[3]

---

[1] With the exception of *conceptual beings*, which do not, strictly speaking, possess an essence (see above, p. 192, note).

[2] *Essentia dicitur secundum quod per eam et in ea res habet esse.* St. Thomas, *De Ente et Essentia*, i.

[3] *Quidditas est ipsa rei entitas considerata in ordine ad definitionem explicantem quid illa sit. Entitas vero rei considerata in ordine ad esse, dicitur* essentia ; *in ordine ad operationem dicitur* natura.

etc., ending with *Gyp* or *Fido*, we may not know what concept (*canine? dog? poodle?*) designates (in the totality of its properties) the essence of *Gyp* or *Fido*. This, however, does not alter the fact that somewhere in the series of concepts in the list just given, and any others which might be inserted among them, there must necessarily be a concept which designates that essence. (In fact, in the example we have chosen, it is the concept *dog*, as zoology discovers by indirect signs, and without being able to give us a truly distinct knowledge of the essence thus apprehended.)

When we think of *man*, for example, or any other object directly presented to the mind by a human idea (an *abstract* idea), we put before ourselves something stripped of individuality, something which, being apprehended by a single concept, constitutes in our mind a single, and solitary object of thought—which is therefore in our mind something belonging to one (*man*) and capable of existing in many (in *all men*), that is something *universal*.[1] Thus everything directly apprehended by an idea of our intellect—and consequently the essence of a thing—is in our mind as a universal.

No doubt, considered as it exists in reality, the essence is individuated, for it is then identical with a subject, *Peter* for example, who is himself individual.[2]

[1] See above, p. 159.

[2] If, for instance, I can say *Peter is a man*, it is because the thing (the material object) apprehended under the object of thought *man* is identical with the thing apprehended under the object of thought *Peter*. When I thus proceed from the existence of things in my mind to their existence in reality, I must say that the object of thought *man*, single in my mind, is multiplied in all the individuals in which it is realised and is identical with each.

But this condition of individuality is no part of the very nature or inmost constitution of the essence, does not belong to the essence of Peter as such, to its character as an essence. If indeed the essence considered in itself (*secundum se*) were individual, our intellect could never know it, for everything directly apprehended by an idea of the intellect is apprehended as a universal.

Considered in itself (*secundum se*) the essence is neither universal nor individual. It abstracts from every condition and mode of existence, being purely and simply *what* the object is primarily as intelligible and what the definition expresses. Thus it is equally present in the actual thing, individuated (in order to exist) and, in our mind, universalised (in order to be known). For example, we see a man only in public, therefore in complete dress, whereas in his bedroom he wears pyjamas. Nevertheless the man we know, when we see him in the street, is the same man, because his pyjamas are no more part of his nature than his suit of clothes ; neither belongs to the man considered in himself. Similarly considered in itself the essence is not universal, but neither is it individual ; [1] that is to say, the essence as such, the essence of Peter taken in itself, abstracts from all the characters which distinguish Peter from Paul or John. [2]

[1] *Cf.* Aristotle, *Metaph.*, vii, 8, 1033 b 22 ; 10, 1035 b 14. Here we are speaking only of corporeal things, which alone are immediately accessible to us (being *connatural* to the human intellect), consequently the only things whose essence is directly knowable (otherwise than by analogy) and can be known complete, *i.e.* completely determined.

[2] From all that has been said it follows that, when, for example, we say *Peter and Paul possess the* same *essence or the* same *nature*, the word *same* refers to the essence of *Peter and Paul* as it exists in the mind (for then it is one and the same object of thought), not as it exists in reality

Conclusion XIV.—The essences of things are universal in the mind, and considered in themselves neither universal nor individual.

This proposition is of the first importance. To deny it inevitably involves suspicion of the human intellect, which cannot directly apprehend in its concepts the individual as such ; [1] we shall either demand from it what it cannot give, a knowledge strictly superhuman —intellectual intuition of the individual—or deny its objective reference and fall into subjectivism.

We must therefore bear firmly in mind that to know the essence or nature of anything it is not necessary to know the principles which constitute its individuality,[2] since the essence, considered in itself, is, in fact, nothing individual. Misconception of this fundamental

(for then it is identical with *Peter* and with *Paul*, two different individuals). But since the essence in question is not individual in itself (*secundum se*), in other words is not distinct in *Peter* and in *Paul qua* essence, it follows that it is in *Peter and Paul* such that it can be apprehended by the mind in a single concept and constitute in the mind one and the same object of thought. This is expressed by the statement that the essence *formally universal* in the mind is *fundamentally universal* in things or in reality. (The nature of anything exists in the *mind* either in a condition of logical or formal universality, as, for example, when we say *man is the species of Peter and Paul*, or in a condition of metaphysical or fundamental universality, as when we say *man is mortal*. The term *fundamental* here refers to the *proximate* foundation of universality. When, on the other hand, we say that the nature or essence is fundamentally universal in *reality*, we are speaking of the *remote* foundation of universality).

[1] We are now speaking of things known by our intellect and do not deal with the question how the intellect knows its own individual and material act.

[2] *Cf.* St. Thomas, *De Verit.*, q. 2, a. 4, *ad* 1 : *Intellectus noster singularia non cognoscens propriam habet cognitionem de rebus, cognoscens eas secundum proprias rationes speciei.*

truth is at the bottom of the errors of several great modern metaphysicians, Spinoza, for example, and Leibniz (exaggerated intellectualists), also Bergson and the anti-intellectualists of the present day.

(*a*) The essence of corporeal things is universal in the sense just explained. That is to say, in this category of being there are a multitude of individuals possessing the same essence.

Individuals possessing the same essence, for example, Peter, Paul, and John, are on the same level in respect of primarily intelligible being ; they are essentially equal.

Nevertheless these individuals differ one from another. Peter is *fair, short, and sanguine*, John *dark, tall, and choleric*, etc.[1] Such characteristics peculiar to a particular individual are not derived from the essence. Otherwise they would be identical in all the individuals which by hypothesis possess the same essence. They are therefore non-essential characters.

Nevertheless they are, in fact, unalterable and necessary.[2] If he were not *fair, sanguine*, etc., Peter would no doubt be a man, but he would not be *Peter*. We must therefore conclude that these characteristics have their ground in what the object is necessarily and primarily, but as an individual, or, in what we may term *the individual nature* of the thing. (By individual

[1] We are not now speaking of those purely *contingent* characteristics which distinguish one individual from another, for example *Peter is in* Paris, *Paul in* Rome, *Peter is* rich, *Paul* poor, etc. We are speaking of those characters which arise out of the *constituent being* of the individual, the *innate* characters, which are, radically at least, unalterable.

[2] But in a fashion altogether different from the characters derived from the essence (properties). See below, p. 212, note.

nature we mean incommunicable to any other object or, if you prefer, wholly circumscribed.)

(*b*) In this individual nature we find, as in the essence, the notes *necessary* and *first being*. But, on the other hand, and this is the important point, it is not the necessary and first being of the thing as first principle of intelligibility ; it is not the first principle of intelligibility. The individual characteristics such as *fair*, *sanguine*, etc., are not, as we pointed out, derived from Peter's essence ; they are not required by it. That is to say, they *do not possess in Peter* a principle or ground which requires them by its very notion, or in virtue of what it is, that is to say, of its own intelligibility (as, for example, *rational* requires *capacity for laughter*). Nevertheless, since they are necessarily possessed by Peter, they have their root in Peter, in Peter's individual nature ; they have there a principle.

They must then have as their principle something which does not require them by its very notion, in virtue of its being or of its own intelligibility, something in the notion of which the intellect cannot discover a necessity for these characteristics rather than any others. Therefore, his principle is in itself wholly indeterminate. If neither by its notion nor in virtue of its being or its own intelligibility it requires this rather than that, it is because in itself it has no notion, being, or intelligibility. We are thus led to a principle which of itself is absolutely nothing conceivable, to *first matter* as Aristotle understood it, something which can enter into the constitution of a being, but is not itself a being.

If it be admitted that non-being of this sort is part of all corporeal things, and that when itself individuated by some qualification [1] it is the primary root of their individuality, it is easy to see that the characters which are derived from the individual nature of the thing, since their primary root is the individual matter with the dispositions it happens to possess at the moment when the thing comes into existence, have, as their first principle in the thing, a principle which does not require them by its very notion—for in itself it has neither notion nor intelligibility ; it requires them solely in virtue of the accidental dispositions it happens to possess at a particular moment.

Thus, the individual nature is not the first principle of intelligibility, because it is *by its matter* that it is the principle of the individual characters.[2]

(*c*) We have merely sought to indicate here how the obscure notion of *first matter*, the study of which belongs

[1] In so far as it *materia signata quantitate*. Obviously beings wholly incorporeal or immaterial (*pure spirits*) cannot derive their individuation from first matter. They must therefore be individuated by their essence itself, and each individual in consequence differs from the rest as a *horse*, for example, differs from a *man*, each being by himself a specific essence. For this reason in the order of pure spirits there are no two beings essentially equal. And consequently in the case of pure spirits (but only in their case) the essence is something individual and the concept of complete essence identical with that of individual nature.

[2] To avoid any possible confusion be it observed that an individual nature is not unintelligible in itself. It is first matter that is unintelligible in itself. Though the individual nature is not the first principle of intelligibility, is not the primarily intelligible being of the thing, it is nevertheless the primary principle of its being, for it is the essence as individuated by matter, and is therefore intelligible in itself. That is why an intelligence more perfect than ours, the Divine Mind for example, can know it directly.

to natural philosophy, arises naturally in the mind as soon as it is understood that considered in itself *the essence of corporeal objects is not individual*, a proposition itself demanded by the fundamental axiom of the trustworthiness of the intellect.

We may further point out that since matter, this species of non-being, is present as the ground of individuation (and consequently as the primary root of certain qualifications)[1] only in the individual nature (in Peter's nature as such) and not in the essence (*humanity*), we may regard the essence, the *primary intelligible being*, as free from all the qualifications due to matter as their primary root or as immaterialised being,[2] in other words as *the archetypal being* of the thing,[3]

[1] That is the sense of St. Thomas's dictum : *formae et perfectiones rerum per materiam determinantur* (*De Verit.*, q. 2, a. 2).

[2] Aristotle, *Metaph.*, vii, 7, 1032 b 14 : λέγω δ'οὐσίαν ἄνευ ὕλης τὸ τί ἦν εἶναι.

[3] *Cf.* St. Thomas, *De Ente et Essentia*, ii : *Haec materia* (signata) *in definitione hominis in quantum homo non ponitur ; sed poneretur in definitione Socratis, si Socrates definitionem haberet. In definitione autem hominis ponitur materia non signata* . . . from this it follows :

(i) That Socrates possesses his essence not precisely as *Socrates*, but as *man*, for the essence is that which the definition expresses (*cf. De Verit.*, q. 2, a. 2, *ad* 9) and *Socrates*, as *Socrates*, is indefinable. Socrates's individual nature is the essence of *man* individuated by the *materia signata*.

(ii) That essence taken in the pure state or separately, as for instance when we speak of *humanity* or *the being man*, may be regarded as the *immaterialised being* (stripped of the qualities derived from *materia signata*), or as the *formal being* of the thing as a whole (comprising both matter—not individual—and form). It is in this sense that the ancients gave to the essence (itself comprising the matter—not individual—and the form) the name of *form* (*forma totius*) : *Et ideo humanitas significatur ut forma quaedam. Et dicitur quod est forma totius . . . sed magis est forma quae est totum, scilicet formam complectens et materiam, cum praecisione tamen eorum per quae materia est nata designari* (St. Thomas, *De Ente et Essentia*, 3). It is important to observe that, although the individual matter (e.g. *haec ossa, hae carnes*) is no part of the essence or specific

an ideal being which in the pure state or separately has no existence except in the mind, and exists in reality only as individuated by matter, in the concrete state of the individual nature.

We must therefore conclude that there is nothing more in the individual nature than in the essence from the standpoint of primarily intelligible or archetypal being.[1] From this point of view all individuals of the same species are on the same level of being ; to

nature, on the other hand the unindividuated or common matter (*ossa, carnes*) is part of it. What constitutes man is not the soul alone, but soul and body together. (*Cf.* Aristotle, *Metaph.*, vii ; St. Thomas, *In VII Metaph.*, l. 10, 1492 and 1496, ed. Cathala). This unindividuated or common matter, taken simply as receiving the form and determined by it, and not as the primary root of certain characters (the individual characters) of the subject, is made known to us by the form : *materia cognoscitur per formam, a qua sumitur ratio universalis* (St. Thomas, *loc. cit. Cf. De Verit.*, q. 10, a. 4 & 5, and is part of that which we have here termed the *immaterialised being* (*archetypal being*) or *formal being* of the thing (*forma totius, seu potius forma quae est totum*).

[1] The individual nature contains more (the qualities peculiar to the individual, for example, a particular temperament) than the essence, but only from the standpoint of matter, not from the standpoint of purely intelligible or immaterialised being. The individual characters are no part of that being and add nothing to it in its own order.

Remark in this connection that the individual characteristics (*fair, sanguine*, etc.) from the very fact that they are derived from the matter, are necessary, and unalterable in a totally different sense than are the characters derived from the essence (*properties*). The latter are necessary *de jure*, as derived from a principle constitutive of the essence which demands them in virtue of its very concept ; it is absolutely impossible that Peter should exist without being *mortal*. The individual characters, on the contrary, are only necessary *de facto*, as derived from particular dispositions of the matter which they presuppose. If it is impossible that Peter should exist without possessing a particular temperament, the existence of that characteristic presupposes certain material conditions in virtue of which Peter possesses a particular individual nature, but which are not themselves necessary. Hence these characters can be to a certain extent modified, and are unalterable only in their ground.

know their (universal) essence is to know all there is to know in them, for the being of Peter as *Peter* is no more complete or determinate than the being of Peter as *man*. It is merely more closely circumscribed.

We can now understand how, although the human intellect cannot directly know the being of objects in its individuality, its nature as an intellect is not frustrated on that account, nor does it miss its formal object, for it truly knows the being of things so far as it is primarily intelligible or archetypal being.[1] Hence, though imperfect, it is neither useless nor untrustworthy.

(*d*) Be it observed that the synonyms *essence*, *quiddity*, and *nature*, all of which denote a universal, may be stretched to denote something singular, when we consider the essence (*humanity*, for example) as individuated by matter (in Peter, for instance), or as it possesses in reality a singular mode of existence. Nevertheless, strictly speaking, the term *nature* alone is compatible with the predicate *individual*, whereas the expressions *individual essence* or *individual quiddity* are incorrect.[2]

[1] In all this we have in mind things immediately accessible to us, namely corporeal things, which the human intellect cannot apprehend directly in their individuality, because, since it is obliged to abstract from images its wholly immaterial ideas, it is by that very fact compelled to abstract from that which constitutes the materiality of sense knowledge, namely the individual matter.

As regards immaterial things (*pure spirits*), our intellect is equally incapable of apprehending them in their individuality, but for an entirely different reason ; because pure spirits are not immediately accessible to us, and we can know them only by analogy, not in their essence, and are unable to apprehend their complete essence.

[2] So far at least as the order of corporeal things is concerned. In the order of pure spirits, on the contrary, the essence is individual (see

We have indeed seen that the terms *essence* and *quiddity* are used in reference both to the existence and the definition of anything. The definition, however, can express only the primarily intelligible being of the thing, for it states its constituent elements which are by their very notion principles of intelligibility in it. Hence the definition cannot express the material individuating principles of the thing, and for that reason the individual nature as such is indefinable. Therefore, since the *quiddity, what the object is as definable*, can only consist in the primarily intelligible being of the object, it must be *universal*. Similarly, that in virtue of which anything invites that supreme perfection which consists in existence can clearly be nothing but its immaterialised being. For it is not in virtue of that in it of which the first principle is matter that it invites existence. Its individuality is merely a condition in which it must be in order to exist. And since the *essence, what a thing is*, taken precisely as that in virtue of which it receives existence, can consist in nothing but its immaterialised being, it must be *universal*.

The term *nature*, on the contrary, is used in reference

above, p. 210, note 1). And if we know the essences of spiritual beings after the fashion of a universal, it is because we only know them inadequately and by analogy with the corporeal objects previously known.

The expression *individual nature* is not uncommon in St. Thomas (*cf. De Verit.*, q. 2, a. 5, *natura singularis ; Sum. Theol.*, i–ii, q. 51, a. 1, *natura individui*, etc.). He also uses, though exceptionally, the expression *essentia singularis* (*cf. De Verit.*, q. 2, a. 7). Whatever may be thought of the propriety of the term, in any case St. Thomas understands by it simply *the essence individuated by the matter* (not in Spinoza's sense, *the essence complete, as an essence, only in the individual*).

to the operations which anything is adapted to perform. A thing, however, does not act solely in accordance with its archetypal or primarily intelligible being, but also as it is subject to particular material conditions and possesses a particular individuality. Nothing therefore prevents our diverting the term *nature* from its primary significance to denote secondarily *what a thing is as* individual.

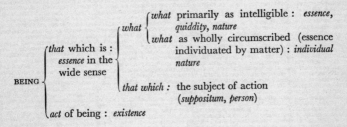

Finally we may remark that in a series of concepts such as *substance, living body, animal, man, Aryan, Breton,* etc., only the concept *man,* strictly speaking, denotes *Peter's essence.* The concepts *substance, living body, animal,* denote only certain elements or intelligible aspects which enter into the constitution of that essence ; in other words, they denote that essence only in one part of its qualifications, and the concepts *Aryan* or *Breton* only as circumscribed and differentiated by certain additional notes arising from the dispositions of matter. *Aryan* and *Breton* are thus, like the essence *man,* universal objects of thought apprehended by the mind in the individual *Peter* and liberated by abstraction from the conditions of individual matter ; but they are universals whose extension is less than that of the essence, and which belong to a particular class (*race*) divided into a multitude of individuals possessing the same essence ; and, since they can be distinguished only by means of characters rooted in certain dispositions of matter they cannot be the subject of a notion strictly speaking distinct, or a true definition.

VI

ONTOLOGY : SUBSTANCE AND ACCIDENT

Adopting the standpoint of intelligibility, we asked ourselves in the preceding paragraph what is the being primarily apprehended by the intellect from that point of view. We were thus brought to the notion of *essence* strictly so-called, or *nature* (the two terms may be regarded as synonymous) ;[1] what an object primarily is as intelligible.

Let us now consider the being of things no longer in reference to intelligibility but in reference to existence.

What from this new standpoint is the being which immediately presents itself to the consideration of the intellect, that to which the latter is directed before anything else ? In other words, what is the being primarily apprehended by the intellect as existing ? We have already answered the question.[2] What the mind apprehends first of all as existing, is beings such as *Peter, Paul, this man, this dog, this bird,* individual concrete and independent subjects, fully equipped to be and to act, and which we have termed *the primary subjects of action, supposita,* or *persons.*[3] It is they who primarily fulfil the act of being.

[1] See above, pp. 201, 213.
[2] See above, p. 195.
[3] The name *person* is reserved for *supposita* of an intellectual nature, who are therefore masters of their actions and possess the maximum of independence,

The subject of action may be thus defined from the standpoint of existence. It exists wholly by itself alone or by its own means, not in the sense that it has no need of a cause (*Peter* has been engendered and many causes combine to keep him in being), but in the sense that it is by itself sufficiently disposed to be drawn from nothingness by the causes of its being ; taken separately it possesses in itself or in its own nature everything necessary to receive existence.[1] In this sense we may say that it is *a being existing by itself* (*per se*) or in virtue of itself, in virtue of its own nature, *ens per se existens*. Since a being of this kind exists as a whole and in no wise as part of another being or subject in which it exists, we may also say that it exists in itself, *in se*.

A being which exists *per se*[2] or rather a being immediately disposed to exist *per se*, is thus from the standpoint of existence the first datum of the intellect. Observe further, that when the intellect makes being of this kind its object, it transcends the limits which define the *essence* in the strict sense or the nature (*what a thing is*, or rather—if we take the pure essence, abstracted from the subject which possesses it—*that in virtue of which an object is what it is*).

We are now concerned, as we have already

---

[1] We are speaking here of created subjects. An uncreated (divine) Person possesses in himself everything necessary to exist with an underived existence. When we say that the *suppositum* is in no way a part of the whole in which it exists, the term *whole* obviously means *a whole that is one in itself* (see p. 250), not a *collective whole*, for example *the universe*.

[2] This formula is preferable, because existence itself cannot enter as a constituent part into the definition of anything created. See further St. Thomas, *Quodlib.*, 2, q. 2, a. 4, *ad* 2 : *ipsum esse non est de ratione suppositi.*

hinted, with *that which* is in the strict sense, *Peter* for example, and not with *that in virtue of which* Peter is what he is (*humanity*, the property of Peter in virtue of which he is a man, or his *individual nature*, the *Petrine humanity*, so to speak, in virtue of which he is Peter).

BEING
$$\begin{cases} \textit{that which is}: \begin{cases} \textit{what (or that in virtue of which)} \\ \textit{essence in the} \\ \textit{wide sense} \quad \textit{that which primarily exists}: \text{ primary} \\ \qquad\qquad \text{subject of action (suppositum, person)} \end{cases} \\ \\ \textit{act of being}: \textit{existence} \end{cases}$$

To be sure, *that which* is, *Peter*, possesses no distinctive characters other than those which constitute *what* he is or his *individual nature*. But when I say *Peter* I conceive this nature as constituting the whole which exists in nothing other than itself.[1] When, on the other hand, I say *Peter's nature*, I conceive that nature as distinct from the whole which it serves to constitute and as existing in him, in that whole.[2] In short, the

[1] Because I conceive it as possessed of a certain mode or fashion of being which philosophers term *subsistence* or *personality*, and which terminates it, somewhat as a point terminates a line.

In this introduction we make no claim to solve the problem of subsistence (the distinction between nature and person) which constitutes one of the most important problems of ontology. Adopting the pedagogical standpoint of coherent exposition, we have merely sought to present and classify notions, so that their sense and mutual relationship may be understood by a synopsis which is complete from the outset.

[2] I conceive it in abstraction from the modality called *subsistence* or *personality* which terminates it. Similarly I can consider a line abstracting from the point which terminates it, in which case the line thus considered is simply a part of the whole constituted by the line and point taken together, and exists in that whole.

subject of action possesses a nature or essence; the concept of that nature or essence taken as such (*what* or *that in virtue of which*) is not the concept of the subject of action (*that which*).

We will now turn to this nature or essence of the subject of action. We have just observed that the subject of action exists (is capable of existence) in virtue of its own nature or its own essence.[1] The nature or essence of the subject of action is therefore that in virtue of which it is capable of existence pure and simple (*simpliciter*); the nature or Peter considered as the subject of action is that in virtue of which I can say simply *Peter exists*.[2]

Existence pure and simple is undoubtedly Peter's primary or first existence. But it is not his sole mode of existence. He is sad to-day, yesterday he was cheerful; to-day he exists as *sad*, yesterday he existed as *cheerful*. He has lost the former existence and acquired the latter, but he has not therefore ceased to exist purely and simply. That is to say, he possesses a host of secondary qualifications in virtue of which he exists not only simply (*simpliciter*) but also under a particular aspect (*secundum quid*). It is thus that he is a *musician* or a *philosopher*, *ill* or *in good health*, *happy* or *unhappy*, etc. All these qualifications have accrued (*accidere*) to that which he is primarily as existing, are increments, or accretions, *accidents*.

Philosophy, health, happiness, sorrow; all these are so

---

[1] In virtue of its *essence* in the strict sense of the term in the case of a purely spiritual subject, in virtue of its nature in the sense of *individual nature* in the case of a corporeal subject. (See p. 235, note 1.)

[2] That is to say, without regard to any particular point of view, without modifying my thought by any addition.

many essences [1] to which our attention has not hitherto been directed, and which are not self-subsistent in being, but on the contrary subsisting, so to speak, only as coverings of the subject of action. Employing the analogy of sensible objects we may say metaphorically that the latter exists beneath the accidents (*substat*) and supports them. From this point of view it may be termed *a substance*.[2] For example, we say that *Peter* is a *substance*. Moreover, since his nature considered precisely as such (*what* he is, *that in virtue of which* he is what he is, that in virtue of which he is capable of existence pure and simple), like himself exists beneath the accidents, it also is entitled to the name of *substance*, and we can speak of *Peter's substance*. We have now distinguished the notion of *substance* as opposed to that of *accident*.[3]

[1] The definition of essence given above (p. 201) is applicable to accidents, if the subject is considered in a particular aspect. Understood in a concrete sense, as attributed to the object (for example *sad* when we say *Peter is sad*), the accident is *what a thing primarily is as intelligible in a particular respect* (*being sad* is the ground on which Peter possesses certain characteristics which necessarily follow from sadness). Understood abstractly, and separately or in the pure state (for instance when we speak of *sorrow*) the accident is *that in virtue of which a thing primarily is what it is as intelligible in a certain respect*.

We may further use the term *essence* no longer in respect of the subject *Peter*, but in respect of the accidents themselves, and say that sorrow is that in virtue of which a particular passion primarily is what it is as intelligible.

[2] The subject of action is also called ὑπόστασις (*hypo-stasis*), πρῶτον ὑποκείμενον, *primum subjectum attributionis*.

[3] Observe that the term *substance* (*substantia*) corresponds to the Greek word οὐσία understood in a restricted sense. The term οὐσία primarily denotes *essence* or *nature*, but since substances are the first object which the intellect attains, when it considers what exists, they are also for that reason the first object which confronts the intellect with the notion of essence ; in other words they are the first to merit the denomination of essence or nature. Hence the term οὐσία, which taken in its most

BEING
- *that* which is : *essence* in the wide sense
  - *what* a thing is (*essence or nature*) and in virtue of which it receives existence
    - in a particular aspect : *accident*
    - absolutely :
  - *that which* primarily exists (the subject of action, *suppositum, person*)
    - } *substance*
- *act* of being : *existence*

SUBSTANCE

The name *substance* is given, as we have just seen, both to the subject of action itself (*that which* primarily exists) and to its nature considered precisely as a *nature or essence* (*what* a thing is, *that in virtue of which* the subject of action is what it is and claims existence pure and simple).[1] What then shall be our definition

general sense denotes *essence*, and is afterwards divided into *substance* and *accident*, has most naturally served to denote in a special sense the first member of the pair, *substance*.

[1] The subject of action (*suppositum* or *person*) is nothing but the substantial nature completed by a particular modality (*subsistence* or *personality*) which terminates it, as a point terminates a line (without adding anything to it in its order of nature) and renders it absolutely incommunicable. The term *substance* (corresponding to the Greek οὐσία, which primarily denotes *essence*—see the preceding note) denotes the *substantial nature* without defining whether or no it is terminated by subsistence. It is therefore applicable alike to the nature (apprehended by the mind without the subsistence which terminates it) and to the subject of action (the *terminated nature*). But when we distinguish and contrast the nature (not terminated) and the subject of action, the term *substance* remains attached to the nature (not terminated) and is then contrasted with the subject of action taken as such. Thus when we speak of *Peter's substance*, we mean precisely *the nature in virtue of which* the subject of action *Peter* possesses primary being, and which is part of him. And theologians use the term in this sense when they teach that in the Divine Trinity the Father and the Son (two distinct Persons) possess the same substance, are *consubstantial*, ὁμοούσιοι.

On the other hand, the Greek term ὑπόστασις (*hypo-stasis*, etymologically the same formation as *sub-stantia*) after a certain vacillation in

of substance ? Being receiving existence of itself (*per se*) or in virtue of itself in the unqualified sense adopted above ? No. For so understood the definition applies only to the subject of action ; absolutely speaking, it alone—*Peter* for example—exists as a whole, and not as part of a being or subject in which it exists. Its nature, on the contrary, is part of itself and exists in itself. Peter's nature exists in Peter, and is part of Peter. It is true that since Peter is himself constituted by it, and exists in virtue of it (*per eam*), this nature does not exist in something previously existing which receives it (as, for example, sorrow exists in Peter, who was previously in existence). We can therefore say that it exists (is capable of existence) *per se*, in the precise sense that in order to exist it has no need to be part of another being previously existing which receives it in itself, but that on the contrary it constitutes the whole (the subject of action) which exists by itself. In this sense and, if we are careful to qualify and explain our meaning, the description *ens per se existens* is applicable not only to the subject of action, but also to its nature, and may therefore serve as the definition of substance.[1]

(The same is true of the expression *ens in se existens*.)

its employment, came finally to denote the subject of action taken as such (*person*) and is used exclusively in this sense. It is thus contrasted with substance understood as *a nature not terminated by subsistence.*

Were we tempted to deny the vital importance of these abstract concepts and distinctions, we might recollect that for the word ὁμοούσιος, on which the true understanding of the Trinity depends, but which differs only by an *iota* from the unorthodox term ὁμοιούσιος, Catholics were willing, when the Arian heresy flourished, to suffer every kind of persecution, and sometimes even death.

[1] *Cf.* John of St. Thomas, *Cursus philos.*, i, *Log.* ii, q. 15, a. 1.

We shall therefore [1] define substance as a thing or nature that can exist by itself or in virtue of itself (*per se*)—and not in another thing (*in alio*), that is to say, in a subject previously existing. [2]

(Alternatively we may define substance as a thing or nature whose property is to exist in itself.)

> *Conclusion XV.*—Substance is a thing or nature whose property is to exist by itself, or in virtue of itself (*per se*) and not in another thing.

It is evident that the idea of substance represents something which really exists. If no substance existed, no nature capable of existing in itself, all natures would be such as could exist only in something else. But in that case, since nature *A* could exist only in nature *B* and nature *B* in turn only in nature *C*, there would be an infinite regression which could never

[1] Existence itself cannot be a constituent part of any created nature. It is for that reason that substance must be defined as *a thing or nature* capable *of existing* per se *or* apt *to exist* per se. The same observation was made above in reference to the *suppositum* (p. 218, note 2).

We must make the sense of the suggested definition clear. If *per se* (or *in se*) is understood in the restricted sense explained in the text, our definition will mean : *substance is a nature apt to exist* per se (*or* in se) qua *nature or essence in the* suppositum *which it constitutes when terminated by the subsistence.* If, however, *per se* (or *in se*) is understood in the absolute sense in which it was taken above (p. 218), the proposed definition will mean : *substance is a nature apt to exist* per se (*or* in se) qua *subject of action* (suppositum *or* person).

[2] The term *substance* signifies *a thing capable of existing in itself, or of subsisting* ; that is to say, of being self-contained as an existent thing (its function *subsistere*), so that, once it exists, it sustains in being the additional qualities or accidents with which it is invested (its function *substare*). But it is only as a *suppositum* that substance is immediately capable of performing these two functions. Considered as a nature or essence it merely seeks to perform them.

reach a nature in which all these natures existed ; they therefore could not exist.

Those philosophers who, like Fichte (nineteenth century), denounced the " dead substance of the Latins " to oppose to it " Teutonic action or becoming " were fighting against the intellect itself, which is simply unable to dispense with the notion of substance and imposes it upon us as an absolutely primary and immediate datum. Moreover, that which they took for substance and declared " dead," " inert," etc., was a mere figment of their own imagination. For substance is not an " empty receptacle," " an inert and dead support." It is the absolutely primal being of a thing, the radical principle of its activity and all its actuality. As Aristotle said, *substantia est primum ens*.[1] But to perceive this a philosopher must make use of his intelligence, rise above the animal life of the senses, and not be content to show his skill in handling words devoid of conceptual content and freighted only with material images.

The substance of an object, so long as that object exists, is as such *immutable*.[2]

Peter's substance is that in virtue of which Peter exists purely and simply, that is to say, as *Peter*. So long as Peter exists, his substance as such cannot change. And when Peter's substance does change (when Peter's *body* becomes a lifeless *corpse*) *Peter* exists no longer, he is dead.

[1] *Metaph.*, vii, 1.
[2] No doubt when Peter grows the change affects Peter's *substance* itself, which increases, but solely in respect of its quantity. It does not affect it as *substance*.

Moreover, in itself substance is *invisible*, imperceptible by the senses. For the senses do not apprehend being as such, but present to us directly only the changing and the moving. In a certain sense, to be sure, it is indeed the substance of Peter that my eyes see, as it was truly Jesus whom the disciples saw at Emmaus, but my eyes thus apprehend the substance only in fact and materially, not formally.

In other words the object seen or touched is something which while seen or touched is at the same time also a substance ; but it is not seen or touched as a substance. As a substance it is conceived, not seen or touched, and so far as it is seen or touched it is coloured or exerting resistance, not being and substance. In the language of philosophy *substance is intelligible in itself* (per se) *and sensible only accidentally* (per accidens). That therefore in things which possesses most importance for us escapes the direct grasp of our senses and imagination, and is a pure object of the intellect, since the intellect alone apprehends being as such (*sub ratione entis*).

Observe that, if from the standpoint of existence substance is in things the being which is the primary and immediate object of the intellect, on the other hand to discover not only that a particular object possesses a substance, but also in what that substance consists, or what is its nature, we are obliged to take our stand upon that which reveals this nature to our senses, namely the operations, phenomena, or accidents, of the substance. In this sense we know the substance by the accidents.

ACCIDENT

Consider now such things as the *laughter*, *movement*, *sorrow*, *joy*, *colour*, etc., which I perceive in *Peter*, and which make *Peter* exist in certain aspects. These things are capable of existence. But they obviously do not exist after the same fashion as substance. To exist they must belong to another being previously existing.[1] They exist as something which belongs to a being or subject already in existence. In this sense we say that they exist in something other than themselves.[2]

> *Conclusion XVI.*—An accident is a nature or essence whose property is to exist in something else.

[1] Previously—if not in the order of time, at least in the order of nature.

[2] The accident of which we are speaking is the *predicamental* accident which is contrasted with the substance. The term *accident*, when it is contrasted with *property* and signifies a *predicate not derived from the essence* (the *predicable* accident) has another meaning.

If we are thinking of the predicamental accident, or of the contrast between substance and accident (a contrast between real beings), we may say that the attribute relates to an *accident* (the intellect in virtue of which a man is *capable of laughter* is an accident really distinct from the substance). If, on the other hand, we are thinking of the predicable accident, that is to say, of the contrast between those unreal beings of logic (the *predicables*), *genus*, *species*, *specific difference*, *property*, and *accident*, it denotes not an accident but a *property*, an attribute predicated of the subject, not as something which helps to constitute his specific essence, but as arising necessarily from it.

Conversely, if we are considering the predicamental accident, we must say that the individuating characteristics (the possession of a particular temperament, or heredity) belong, radically at least, to the substantial, not to the accidental order. If, on the other hand, we are considering the predicable accident, we must say that these characteristics are accidents (attributes predicated of the subject, neither as helping to constitute the specific essence nor as derived from it).

It follows that though an accident partakes, indeed, of being, it does not exist *as* a being ; it is essentially *of* a being, *ens entis*, and capable of existence only as the complement or perfection of a being. Thus the word *being* is predicable of the accident only in a secondary and indirect sense, and whereas *being* in the primary sense of the term is from the standpoint of existence the subject of action, so that our intellect apprehends immediately and of itself the subject of action, the substance, that which exists in itself, we find it difficult to arrive at a clear understanding of the accident. To succeed we are obliged to elaborate our notion of being, to make it more pliable, plane it down, bind it to the real, in short, to apprehend the accident by analogy with the substance which is contrasted with it.

The mere fact that the term *accident* is a *substantive* involves us in the danger of regarding the accident as a substance, a piece of substance or a reduced substance. The imagination intervenes, and we depict to ourselves accidents and phenomena as fragments of matter inlaid in the *suppositum*, like a casing of mosaic or marquetry. Those for whom the words *accident* or *phenomenon* evoke images of this kind miss the notion of accident altogether. They conceive in fact only pseudo-substances and are incapable of advancing a step further in philosophy. An original effort of the intellect elaborating the notion of being is here the sole remedy.

It is obvious that things such as an act of thought or a movement of emotion cannot be confused with our substance, because they come and go, and change within us, whereas our substance never ceases or changes, being as such immutable so long as we exist. Nevertheless these things are realities which affect us intrinsically. They are, therefore, really distinct from the substance in which they exist or, in technical language, *inhere*. There are thus *contingent* accidents (such that the subject can exist without them) real and really distinct from the substance.

But if change, by showing that there are in a subject things which come and go, helps us to arrive at the notion of accident, it is very far from being a necessary attribute possessed by every accident. There are things without which a subject cannot exist, and which nevertheless are accidents, additional beings which complete the substance; our understanding itself, for example, and our will are evidently something real in us. But they cannot be confused with our substance. For we possess a distinct notion of them wholly extrinsic to that of substance,[1] which would be impossible if they were not essentially different from the latter.[2] Therefore the understanding and the

[1] We distinctly conceive the understanding or intellect as a faculty of knowing whose object is being, the will as a faculty of conation whose object is the good, substance as a nature or essence whose specific property is self-subsistence. The three concepts fall wholly outside each other.

[2] We are able to reason in this way because we are dealing with things proportionate to our intellect, which apprehends them by a proper and distinct concept (things which are, we say, known by their essence). In such cases, if two concepts are wholly external to each other, it is because the things they present to the mind really differ one from the other. Otherwise our intellect would deceive us. It is in this way that we prove that quantity or extension is an accident really distinct from corporeal substance, and that in every created thing the essence is really distinct from the existence. (On the latter point see John of St. Thomas, *Cursus Phil.*, *Phil. Nat.*, q. 7, a. 4.) When, however, the distinction is due to the standpoint from which the mind

will are real things in us distinct from our substance, consequently accidents (belonging as we shall see later to the category of *quality*). There are, therefore, *necessary* accidents (without which the subject cannot exist) real and really distinct from the substance.

The different schools which profess conflicting doctrines on the problem of substance may be represented roughly by the following scheme :

Philosophy of Aristotle and St. Thomas

There are as many substances as there are individuals. In virtue of its substance each of these possesses primary being, but there are in each real accidents really distinct from the substance.

Substantialists	*Phenomenalists*
There are no real accidents really distinct from the substance, which is the sole reality.	There is no substance ; the accidents which are apparent to the senses or the consciousness (phenomena) are the sole reality.
Descartes, Leibniz, and especially Spinoza. The German pantheists of the nineteenth century.	English sensationalists— neo-Kantian school. Philosophy of pure becoming.

Descartes denied the existence of real accidents really distinct from the substance. He identified corporeal substance with extension and the substance of the soul with the act of thought. He thus set

views the same object we have indeed two distinct concepts, but not wholly external one to the other. For example, I distinguish in *Peter* his being a *man* and his being an *animal*, though in reality they are one and the same being. But the concept *man*, far from being external to the concept *animal*, implies it on the contrary.

philosophy on a path which could only lead to pantheism (for if there are no accidents distinct from substance, every substance is its action—a perfection which belongs to God alone—and the concept of substance becomes identical with that of absolute Being or God, with whom everything is thus confused), or if pantheism is to be avoided, to the denial of substance, which such a philosophy will do its utmost to disprove and to banish from the human intellect.

Spinoza erected on the Cartesian foundation a *monism* or absolute pantheism from which Leibniz attempted in vain to escape by substituting for the single substance of Spinoza an infinite multitude of individual substances (*monads*), thus in effect replacing Spinoza's God by a boundless host of deities. Though they rejected the notion of *substance*, for which they substituted that of *becoming* or *evolution*, and regarded the *thing-in-itself* not as an object which imposes itself on the mind but as a background of the mind which produced the object, the German metaphysicians in the succession of Kant (Fichte, Schelling, Hegel) may be ranked among the exponents of pantheistic *substantialism* since they posited a single principle which constitutes by its development the stuff and reality of all things.

In the phenomenalist camp the English *sensationalists* and *associationalists* maintained that *states of consciousness* (sensations, emotions, ideas, etc.) are the sole reality accessible to us, and attempted to reduce the whole of psychology to the mutual association of these states of consciousness. The philosophers of pure becoming (Bergson, in particular, who thus joins hands with

Heraclitus over a gulf of twenty-five centuries) deny the existence of anything permanent in things, and maintain that change without any subject of change is the sole reality. (In psychology these philosophers are opposed to the former group inasmuch as they substitute " a continuous stream of consciousness " (W. James) for a mosaic or " host " of states of consciousness. But they are agreed in rejecting the notion of substance.)

Kant (eighteenth century) substituted for the distinction between substance and accidents in things (substance and accidents being equally objects of knowledge, the former by means of the second) [1] an opposition of two separate worlds, the world of things as they are in themselves (*things-in-themselves*, *noumena*) and the world of phenomena manufactured by our mind. He regarded the thing-in-itself as wholly unknowable, though he affirmed its existence. This thing-in-itself, sought now in the subject of knowledge, became all in all to the German pantheists of the nineteenth century. Renouvier and the French neo-Kantians, on the contrary, taught that the thing-in-itself, the substance, is not merely unknowable but absolutely non-existent, and the concept of it chimerical.

The various phenomenalist philosophers just mentioned failed to perceive that what they really deny is the accident, not the substance. What they understood by *phenomena* is a mere pseudo-substance expressed by a concept ashamed of itself and self-contradictory, a substance pulverised, melted down, emptied of real subsistence, something which is not accident, but

[1] See above, p. 226.

232

being of a being, the pure complement of being, and inconceivable except as correlated with substance. Since they have never really understood what is meant by substance, and posit, under the appellation of *phenomena,* pseudo-substances, they quite naturally refuse to admit another substance behind these pseudo-substances of their imagination.

THE INDIVIDUALITY OF SUBSTANCE

The being primarily apprehended by the intellect from the standpoint of existence (the *substance*) is something *individual.* The intellect indeed apprehends it as individual, for it apprehends the being of things only by turning to the sensations and images which reveal things to us under the conditions of their existence and in their individuality. Moreover, that alone can really exist which is by nature a completely circumscribed and self-contained unit, or an individual.

(*a*) Our intellect, it is true, can have no direct knowledge of this substance in its individuality ; it simply knows, by turning to the images from which it derives its ideas, that this substance is individual, it does not know in what its individuality consists ; Peter's substance is directly revealed to it only by a universal idea. Peter's *substance* thus perceived, in abstraction from his individuality, is simply Peter's *nature* apprehended in the characters which constitute his *essence,* strictly speaking. And since we say of *man* that he *moves, laughs, possesses understanding and will,* etc., as we say it (primarily and in the first place) of *Peter* or *Paul*—since in consequence the property of existing beneath the accidents, which strictly belongs

233

to the subject and his individual nature, is thence transferred to the nature of the subject stripped of its individuality by abstraction—we shall also give the name of *substance*, though in a secondary sense (*substantia secunda*), to Peter's nature, as apprehended in abstraction from his individuality, that is to say, *the universal essence* man *or* humanity. On the other hand, by substance in the primary sense (*substantia prima*), we shall understand the *individual substance*.[1]

It is now clear that when we consider the being primarily apprehended by the intellect in material things we stress either the individual being or the universal being according as we consider this being primarily apprehended in relation to existence or in relation to intelligibility.

In relation to intelligibility the being primarily apprehended in things by the intellect is the essence, strictly speaking, which in itself is not individual and exists in the mind in a condition of universality ; and it is only in an improper sense that the term *essence* is used of the essence individuated by the individual matter (that is, of the *individual nature*).

In relation to existence, on the contrary, the being primarily apprehended in things by the intellect is

---

[1] In the Aristotelian and Scholastic vocabulary the term *substantia prima*, οὐσία πρώτη, denotes (see above note) the *individual nature* of the subject of action without determining whether or no it is terminated by subsistence. Usually indeed it does in fact denote the *terminated nature*, or subject of action, the *hoc aliquid*. It does not, however, denote formally the subject of action taken as such and contrasted with the (non-terminated) nature. That function belongs to the terms *suppositum* and *persona* (ὑπόστασις).

Remark that the distinction between the subject of action and the nature (non-terminated by the subsistence) is in the main due to the Schoolmen. Aristotle himself did not make it explicitly.

the individual substance,[1] and it is in a secondary sense that the term *substance* is used of the nature stripped of its individuality by abstraction (that is, of the essence in the strict sense).[2]

Here we may call to mind what was said above [3] about the individual nature. We see at once how we should classify the different concepts with which we have made acquaintance hitherto.[4]

BEING
- *that* which is : *essence* in the wide sense
  - what the sub-ject is
    - primarily as intelligible (*essence* in the strict sense) and *in virtue of which* it exists
      - in a particular respect : *accident*
      - absolutely : *substantia secunda*
    - primarily as completely circumscribed (*individual nature*) and *in virtue of which* it exists as such
      - *substantia prima*
  - *that which* primarily is : the primary subject of action (*suppositum, person*)

  substance

- *act* of being : *existence*

---

[1] Taken precisely as that in virtue of which the subject possesses its first being, the substance, *substantia prima*, is the *subject's individual nature*. We said above (p. 214) that that in virtue of which a thing is susceptible of existence is the universal essence, the reason being that we were then considering precisely what is the ground on which a thing is susceptible of existence, in contrast with that which is merely a condition or state in which it must be in order to exist. Here, however, we are dealing with that in which the existence of the thing considered precisely as in the state necessary in order to exist is grounded, and this is not the universal essence, but the individual nature of the subject.

[2] Hence in the order of pure spirits and there alone (where no distinction exists between the individual nature and the essence, see above p. 211, n. 3 ; p. 213, n. 2), the substance in the primary sense of the word is also the essence, strictly speaking. In the material order, on the other hand, substance in the primary sense of the word is the subject's individual nature, and it is only in a secondary sense that the essence, strictly speaking, is called *substance*.   [3] See page 209.

[4] *The* quod *and the* quo. We have already observed (see above, p. 200, note 1) that the essence taken in the concrete or as attributed

(*b*) *Per se, a se, in se.* We have defined *substance* as *a thing whose property it is to exist by itself* (per **se**) *or in itself* (in se). We must determine carefully the exact sense of these expressions.

A thing is said to exist in itself (*in se*) when it does not exist as part of a whole previously existing, but

to the thing (*what* a thing primarily is as intelligible) is not presented to the mind in its purity ; it is in fact presented to the mind together with the thing or subject which it determines. To possess it in its purity, it must be conceived separately, without the thing or subject it determines, as for instance when we speak of *humanity* or, to force language, of *the being man, the entity man.* In that case it must be defined as *that in virtue of which* a thing primarily is what it is as intelligible, or, in other words, that in virtue of which a thing is constituted in a particular degree of being primarily intelligible. For this reason it will be better to substitute in our synopses for the term *what* the phrase *that in virtue of which.* So we finally get the following table :

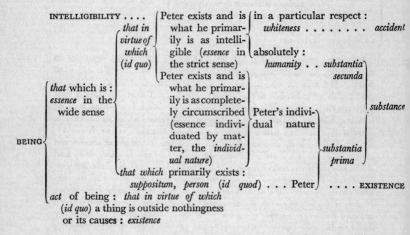

The distinction between the *quod* and the *quo* plays a part of the first importance in the metaphysical analysis of things.

itself constitutes the whole which exists. In this sense Peter exists in himself.

A thing is said to exist by itself or in virtue of itself (*per se*), when it is brought into existence in virtue of itself, or of its own nature (by the causes on which it depends, if it is a created nature). In this sense Peter exists *per se*.[1]

Philosophy makes frequent use of this expression, *per se*. It always means *in virtue of itself, in virtue of its own essence* (*per suam essentiam*)—whether the quality under consideration forms part of the essence of the thing or necessarily results from it as its principle (in which case *per se* is opposed to *per accidens*)[2] or whether we merely wish to state that the attribute under consideration immediately pertains to the thing which does not receive it through the intermediary of anything other than its own essence (in which case *per se* is opposed to *per aliud*). It is in this sense that the subject of action exists *per se*, whereas the accident exists *per aliud*.

But the expression *per se* does not mean *in virtue of itself or of its own nature as the absolutely first principle or as the complete and ultimate explanation*. This is something totally different, which is expressed by the phrase *a se, of* or *from itself* (as opposed to *ab alio*). That which is *a se* is evidently *per se*, but that which is *per se* is not

---

[1] Existence *per se* or *in se* can, we have already seen (see pp. 218, 223), be ascribed, as it is understood in a more or less strict sense, either to substance in general (that which exists *per se* and *in se* contains in itself whatever is necessary in order to receive existence and is not part of a *previously existent* whole) or exclusively to the subject of action (*suppositum* or *person*, which contains in itself *everything* necessary in order to receive existence, and exists *in no respect* as part of a whole).

[2] For example, Peter is *per se* alive, endowed with intellect, and the faculty of laughter, the artist is *per se* one who fashions objects. But Peter is *per accidens* a sufferer from influenza or the heir to a large fortune, the artist *per accidens* celibate or married, etc.

by any means for that reason *a se*. That which exists
a se or from itself, possessing in itself the entire explanation of its existence, is uncaused ; God alone is from
himself, *a se*. Created substances on the contrary
(*created subjects of action*) are caused ; they exist *per se*,
in virtue of their essence ; they do not exist *a se*.
In their own nature they possess everything necessary
to receive existence, but not to possess an existence
not received from without. They are sufficient by
themselves to exist, in the strictly qualified sense that
they do not exist as something which belongs to something else, but, absolutely speaking, they are by no
means a sufficient ground of their own existence.
That which is *a se* cannot cease to exist ; that which is
per se without being *a se* can lose its existence.

The distinction between that which exists *a se* and
that which exists *per se* is perfectly clear. Nevertheless
certain philosophers have lost sight of it, notably
Spinoza, who ascribes *aseity* (*a-se-itas*) to every
substance. (From which it follows immediately that
there is only one substance, and that everything
is God—monism and pantheism). When indeed
Spinoza defines substance as *that which is in itself and
is conceived by itself*, he really means, as the context
shows,[1] *that which to be and to be conceived needs absolutely
nothing except itself*. Descartes had already defined
substance ambiguously as *res quae ita exsistit ut nulla
alia re indigeat ad exsistendum, a thing which exists in such
a fashion that it has need of nothing else in order to exist.*[2]

[1] *Cf. Ethics*, i, 7.   [2] *Principia Philosophiae*, i, 51.

VII

ONTOLOGY : ACT AND POTENTIALITY

WHEN we studied being first from the standpoint of intelligibility, then from that of existence, we saw that the object primarily apprehended by the intellect, *being* in the primary sense of the term, was in the former case what we call *essence*, in the latter what we call *substance*.

We must now consider the being of things (understanding the term *being* in its most general and indeterminate sense) from the standpoint of *action*, in reference to the manner in which things behave in reality, or, if you prefer, in reference to what they do. This new standpoint acquaints us with a third primary sense of the term being.

(*a*) What is the first truth which the intellect grasps as soon as it has formed the notion of being ? It is sufficient to consider the notion to see at once that what is, is (principle of *identity*), or again that what is, cannot not be at the same time and in the same relation (principle of *non-contradiction*). That is to say, that everything is what it is, that it is not what it is not, and that it is everything that it is.

We will now consider what things do, what is their natural behaviour, what is the primary fact of experience grasped by the senses and consciousness. Things change. The arrow flies, the animal runs, what was cold becomes hot under the action of fire, food becomes flesh, what was living dies, and every spring that which had no being comes into existence.

Although, like all our primary notions, it is very difficult to explain scientifically, everybody knows by experience in what this great fact of *change* or *motion* consists. We may say that wherever there is change there is a transition (from one being to another, or from one mode of being to another). And for transition to exist, there must be something which undergoes it, something which is the subject of change, for example a subject which ceases to be in a particular place or a particular thing (*terminus a quo, the arrow pressed to the bow, the food, the seed*), to be in another place or another thing (*terminus ad quem, the arrow in the target, flesh, the mature plant*).

There is no change without a subject which is changed, and which must be some particular thing before the change is effected [1]—in other words being is prior to change.

Those, indeed, who maintain that change is prior to being, and that there is change without a subject which is changed and which is some particular thing before the change is effected, deny the principle of identity and fall into absurdity. For when they take up this position, they must either continue to accept the notion of *being*, in which case to affirm that there is change without a subject of change, or that change is prior to being, is to affirm that what has no being

---

[1] For example, in a substantial change the first matter, which is not a being, but potential being, is the subject which is changed and constitutes a particular body, or particular being, by its union with a particular substantial form, before it constitutes some other body by its union with another substantial form.

changes, which is manifestly absurd ; or they must reject the notion of being as illusory and argue that instead of conceiving *being* we must conceive *change*, in which case they must reject as false, together with the notion of *being*, the principle of identity which is bound up with it, and maintain that thought is essentially deceptive, which is equally absurd.

We are, therefore, absolutely obliged to hold that being is prior to change, and that there is no change without a subject which is changed, and which is some particular thing before it changes ; or, in the language of philosophy, that *there is no motion without a subject which is moved.*

(*b*) We will now turn away from experience and every sensible representation and attempt to consider change with our intellect, that is to say, in terms of being, the formal object of the latter. We shall inquire how or in what respect the starting-point of change can thus become the goal. You will answer, perhaps, that it is according as it is this or that, in respect of what it is, that the starting-point becomes the goal. But the starting-point is nothing but what it is, and is already everything that it is, and therefore in this respect is incapable of becoming, for it already is. You may then say that it is according as it is not this or that, in respect of what it is not, that the starting-point becomes the goal. But in respect of what it is not, the thing is nothing whatever, is pure nothing, and therefore cannot be the source of the product of change. It is incapable of becoming, for it simply is not.

Hence the starting-point of change cannot become its goal—either in respect of what it is or in respect of what it is not.   In other words, the new being which is the product of change can be derived neither from the being which already exists, nor from a nothing, which has no existence whatever.   Is change, therefore, impossible, as Parmenides maintained ?   And are we obliged with him to deny the evidence of our senses, which witnesses to the fact of change ?

(c) No.   But we are obliged to develop and explore our idea of being.   Evidently in the analysis we have just made something has been left out.   The starting-point of change is no doubt already everything which it is, but it is not yet all which it can be ; it is not yet that particular thing it is destined to become, but it possesses the means to be it, it can be it.   Therefore between being and not being there is the *power of being*. It is neither in respect of what it is, nor in respect of what it is not, but in respect of what it can be that the starting-point of change becomes its goal.

The arrow is here (*on the bow*, for instance) and from the standpoint of *being* pure and simple, it is nowhere else ; but it can be there (*at the goal*, for example), and possesses the means to be there.   Bread is bread and nothing but bread, and not flesh, so far as it is, in the sense of *being* pure and simple, that is to say, of *being* completely realised ; but it can cease to be bread and become flesh.   There is in it that which enables it to undergo the change under the action of certain determinate causes.

POTENCY OR POTENTIALITY

Things therefore are not confined and held fast by what they are and what they are not.   Even while they are here and not there, this and not that, they possess the power to be there and no longer here, that and no longer this. But so long as they are here or are this, that power which they possess remains mere power and is not manifested.

This power in them is as such something real. Consider a man asleep. He neither sees nor speaks nor walks. But he is not therefore blind, paralysed, or dumb. He is really capable of seeing, speaking, and walking. While he does not speak he retains the power to speak, he has it in him ; whereas he cannot without a violation of nature become a tree or a bird. Or again take a billiard ball at rest. It is immobile (not moving). But it is not therefore immovable. It is really capable of motion. While it does not move, it retains the power of being moved, it has it in itself ; whereas it has no natural power of passing through a wall. The power of being is not *being* in the full and primary sense of the term ; but power of being without as yet being is not sheer *nonentity*. *Power of being* taken precisely as such is irreducible either to *nonentity* or to *being* pure and simple. It is something different from either, something *sui generis* for which philosophy must find a place. Precisely so far as things can be something they are not, they, after an inferior fashion, are.

We have thus found something which does not deserve to be called being, on which that title can be bestowed only in a secondary and improper sense, as an alms, so to speak, but which nevertheless is real. It is what philosophers term *potency* or *potentiality*.

In using the term *potency* we must be on our guard against ambiguity. This potency is not that of which

243

we think when we say that a being *is potent*. This potency is not an active power; power to effect something or to work, at least when understood as active, is the absolute contrary of the power or potency with which we are now concerned, being not *potency* but *act*. The potency of which we are speaking is entirely passive, nothing more than a real power of being or becoming. Wax is *in potency* to receive the impress of the seal, water *in potency* to become ice or vapour. The active powers (for instance, the faculties of the soul) are also rightly termed *potencies* or *potentialities*, but only in so far as they are not, or are capable of not being, actually operative, or so far as they are simple capacities of action or operation.

ACT

Since, however, power of being, though not nothing, is not being in the full and primary sense of the term, we must find a name for *being* in the full and primary sense of the term as distinguished from *potentiality*. Philosophers call it *act*.

Here also we must beware of ambiguity. We are not concerned, at least not primarily and chiefly, with an *act* in the ordinary sense of the word, with *doing* or *action*. *Action* or operation is indeed an act, *being in act*, but it is what is termed the *secondary act* (*actus operationis*). Action presupposes being. And the *primary act* is the act of being (*actus exsistentiae*), moreover of being a particular thing (*actus essentiae*). For example, a body is luminous *in act*, even when it is not illuminating anything else. Clay, once modelled, is a statue *in act*, water at 32° Fahrenheit is ice *in act*, and the moment anything effectively is one thing or another and especially the moment anything exists, it is *in act*.

Act may therefore be defined as *being* in the strict sense of the term, taken in the fullness thus signified, or again the finished, the *determinate*, or the *perfect* as such. *Potentiality*, on the other hand, is the *determinable*, the *perfectible*, that which is capable of being finished, as such ; not a being but a real power of being.

We must take care not to attempt to think with our imagination these concepts of act and potentiality. They can be thought by the intellect alone. Least of all must we conceive of potentiality as some sort of being in act which we imagine as more or less hazy, indefinite, inactive, and hidden in the object. Potentiality in itself is absolutely incapable of being represented. It is not a spring or an organ hidden in the thing, nor a character prefigured in it after the fashion of an imaginary statue outlined beforehand by the veins of marble within the block, nor yet an act thwarted or rendered abortive, like an effort or pressure overcome by the resistance of an obstacle. It is absolutely nothing done or in process of doing, absolutely nothing in act. In itself it cannot be conceived (for in that case it would necessarily be conceived as something determinate). It can be conceived only by means of the act (the particular thing) with which it is correlated, as the simple power of being that particular thing.

Conclusion XVII.—*Being*, considered in relation to the fullness and perfection which the term signifies, is divided into *being* in the strict sense or *act*, and *power of being* or *potentiality*.

We are now in a position to understand *change*. The product of change arises neither out of being in act nor out of nothing, but from potential being. In other words, the action of the efficient cause draws, *educes*, from the potentiality of the subject the determination, the *form*, which was wanting in the starting-point of the change and characterises its goal, as when the action of fire educes from the potentiality of water (the water is cold, but can be hot) the determination (a specific intensity of heat) which characterises it as the result of the change. The *change* is the transition from potentiality to act, or, more accurately, according to a definition to which we must return later, it is *the act of a thing in potentiality taken precisely in respect of its potentiality : actus exsistentis in potentia prout in potentia.*

ACT AND POTENTIALITY IN THINGS

From what has been said it follows that all changeable things, in whatever respect they are subject to change, are compounded of potentiality and act. God alone, since he is absolutely unchangeable, is devoid of any potentiality. Since he is subsistent Being itself or the Fullness of being, he is incapable of becoming ; there is no perfection which he does not possess or rather is not already ; he is pure act.

The being of all other things, on the contrary, is too poor and too weak to realise simultaneously everything they are capable of being. For every one of them there is really open a vast range of possibilities, of which they can never realise more than a few, and that by changing.

Here we may observe that the obscure and mysterious concept of first matter whose acquaintance we made when we studied the notion of individual nature is that of a pure potentiality in the order of substance, which can be any and every body and by itself is none. It is the purely potential principle which in union with an actual principle (a *substantial form*) constitutes a particular corporeal substance, and is the subject of substantial changes.

Potentiality and act divide between them the totality of created being, both in the order of substance and in the order of accidents. In other words, they are, like being itself, *transcendental* objects of thought which exceed or transcend every limitation of class or category, and include all created things. The substance of bodies is compounded of potentiality (*first matter*) and act (*substantial form*). The substance of incorporeal things (*pure spirits*) is not composite; it is in respect of that which constitutes its nature or essence wholly *act*. But it is not therefore *pure act* (in the case of pure created spirits), for this substance (*substantial essence*) is itself potentiality in relation to that which is the ultimate act of everything real (*actualitas omnis formae*) or existence : pure spirits do not derive their existence from themselves, *a se* ; they can not be.

On the other hand, we may remark that every accident (*whiteness, strength, virtue*, etc.) is an act (*accidental form*) which determines the subject and is itself sometimes in potentiality in respect of further determinations. The intellect, for example, is an

247

accident (an *accidental form*) whose subject is the soul, and it is in potentiality in respect of a particular act of thought.

It is clear that all the notions with which we have become acquainted hitherto can be classified in the following fashion :

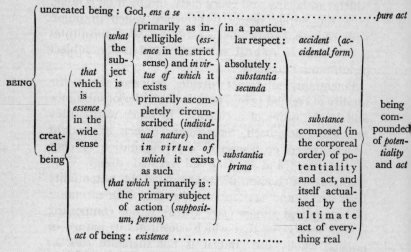

After what has been said, it is sufficient to consider the notions of potentiality and act to see immediately the truth of the following *Axioms* :

(i) *Potentiality cannot exist in the pure state, apart from any act.* This is evident. For, since existence is an act, potentiality can only exist in beings which are in some other respect in act.[1]

---

[1] Hence first matter cannot exist separately unactualised by some particular substantial form. Similarly essence is in relation to the **act** of existence a potentiality really distinct from existence but actual in virtue of existence.

(ii) *Nothing is educed from potentiality to act except by some being in act.* It is plainly impossible that that which is in potentiality, that which is capable of having a determination or a perfection but does not have it, should give to itself what it lacks, so far as it does not possess it, that is to say, so far as it is in potentiality.

(iii) *Act is prior to potentiality.* A consequence of the preceding axiom.[1]

(iv) *Potentiality is essentially relative to act* and is for the sake of the act (*potentia dicitur ad actum*). It is indeed only in relation to the act that the potentiality can be conceived (only in relation to *being white* that we can conceive the *power of being white*) ; and it is also only for the determination or perfection that the determinable and the perfectible as such are.

(v) *Act and potentiality belong to the same order ;* that is to say, both must be in the order of substance, or both in the order of accident. For it is evident that every act which at the same time completes and specifically determines a potentiality must belong to the same order as that potentiality. The activity of thought, for example, belongs to the order of accident like the faculty itself from which it proceeds and which is in potentiality to that activity.

(vi) *Everything acts according to its nature in act.*

---

[1] This axiom is the metaphysical explanation of the truth previously affirmed : *being is prior to becoming or change.* Absolutely speaking this is true. In the order of material causality on the other hand potentiality is prior to act, becoming prior to being, the seed prior to the tree. But the seed itself presupposes the tree which produced it and at the beginning of the entire process the actuality of the First Cause.

Since activity is an act (*actus operationis*) which is brought into being by the subject from which it proceeds it presupposes (as laid down by *Axiom ii*) that the latter is in act to the extent to which it produces that activity. The same truth differently enunciated is expressed by the dictum *action or operation manifests being* (*operatio sequitur esse*).

(vii) *The combination of two beings in act cannot produce something which is one of itself.* We call *one of itself* (*unum per se*), as opposed to *one by accident*, a thing which constitutes a single being and not a conjunction of beings, in other words a thing which is one in virtue of the nature by which it exists. For example, a living organism is a unit of itself, whereas a machine or a house is an accidental unit.[1] This distinction once understood, it is plain that two beings in act, and as such constituting two beings, can never by their combination constitute anything except a conjunction of beings, that is to say, an accidental unit.[2]

Once more on this question of act and potentiality we find philosophers divided into three great schools. The school of *Aristotle and St. Thomas* teaches the distinction between potentiality and act, the priority

[1] No doubt, if you destroy the unity of the machine or the house, you destroy the machine or the house, but you do not destroy the *natures* (or *substances*) of which it is composed (*iron, steel, bricks*, etc.). Destroy, on the other hand, the unity of an organism, you destroy its very nature (*substance*).

[2] This axiom plays an important part in natural philosophy and particularly in psychology. For instance, the Cartesian conception which regards the soul and the body as independent of each other, two complete substances, is unable to explain the substantial unity of the human being, because two complete substances are two beings in act.

of act to potentiality, the reality of motion and becoming, but the priority of being to motion. It also shows that between God (the pure act) and all things besides (compounds of potentiality and act) there is an absolute and infinite difference.

Exaggerated intellectualism (Parmenides, Spinoza, Hegel) refuses to admit the notion of *potentiality*, because by itself it is obscure. If, however, everything which is, is wholly act or pure act, either motion must be unreal (Parmenides) or contraries identical (Hegel) and creatures must possess the same nature as God (pantheism).

Anti-intellectualism (Heraclitus, Bergson) equally rejects the distinction between *potentiality* and *act*, but because the notion of *being* is in the opinion of these philosophers illusory. If, however, *being* is denied in favour of *becoming* or *pure change*, *pure act* can no longer exist; and however the exponents of this school may struggle to escape the logic of their position, God must possess the same nature as things (pantheism).

Moderate Intellectualism
(*School of Aristotle and St. Thomas*)

Potentiality and act in things. God or the pure act is absolutely distinct from created things.

Exaggerated Intellectualism	*Anti-intellectualism*
No potentiality in things. Everything is absorbed either in pure being, or in the contradiction which constitutes becoming, and created things are identified with God.	Neither act nor being. Everything is absorbed in change or pure becoming, and God is identical or continuous with things.

Material and formal, virtual and formal (or *actual*), *implicit and explicit, in accomplished act, in express act.*

251

In connection with the notions of potentiality and act philosophers use certain expressions whose meaning must now be explained.

We have just learned the meaning of the two correlatives *in potentiality* and *in act*. The marble before it has been carved is a statue *in potentiality*; as soon as the sculptor has given it the form he intends, it is a statue *in act*.

(*a*) Closely related to these expressions *in potentiality* and *in act* are the expressions so frequently met in philosophy *material* and *formal*. They have been borrowed from natural philosophy (cosmology) which proves that every corporeal substance is compounded of two principles, *first matter* (pure potentiality in the order of substance) and *substantial form* or first act.[1]

The terms *material* and *formal* have passed from natural philosophy into all branches of philosophy, to designate, by analogy, on the one hand whatever, in itself indeterminate and potential, plays the part of a subject which receives a determination, on the other hand whatever possesses of itself a determining, actualising, and specificatory function, or ag in whatever is taken as possessing a particular character, in a particular aspect. It is in this sense that, as we have already seen,[2] we distinguish between the material and formal objects of a virtue, science, or faculty.

Hence arises in particular the distinction between the material and formal statement. We speak *materially* when we do not take the things of which we speak precisely as possessing the characters denoted by the words we use; we speak *formally* when in the

---

[1] See above, pp. 166–168. [2] See above, p. 106.

things of which we speak we consider not so much the subject which possesses these characters as the characters themselves, with the sharp contour and clear-cut line they describe in it. This distinction is extremely important. Formal statement should, indeed, be the constant aim of philosophy ; and, on the other hand, many propositions are true *formaliter loquendo* which are false *materialiter loquendo*, and vice versa. For examples the following propositions are true understood formally, but false if understood materially :

Everything which is, is good (so far as it is).

The common good is always preferable to the good of the individual (provided the common good is understood formally, in which case the union of the soul with God, that is with the transcendent common good of all creatures, is to be preferred to everything else).

Superiors ought always to be obeyed. (So far as they are *superiors*, and command nothing opposed to the orders of a superior of higher rank.)

There are men who are natural slaves. (If slave is understood formally, as meaning *destined for manual or servile work.*)

Every virtue is stable. (If we consider solely its quality of *virtue.*)

Knowledge is infallible (so far as it is *knowledge*).

Conversely, the following propositions are true only in a certain context, and if understood materially.[1]

---

[1] It would be of interest to show how philosophy, since it has given up the technical language of Scholasticism, has increasingly tended to use terms in a material rather than a formal sense. Hence a number of badly stated problems, and a host of misunderstandings both between

This picture is the Adoration of the Magi.
This book is the philosophy of Pythagoras.
Speech has been given to man to conceal his thoughts.
Philosophy is proud.
The British Constitution is good because it is illogical.

(*b*) We must be careful to distinguish *in potentiality* from *virtual,* for they signify entirely different things.[1] A thing is said to be *virtual,* or to *exist virtually,* when it is contained in another thing of superior rank, not in its being or proper determination (its *formality*) but under another being or determination (another formality), so that it is truly there according to the *virtue* or degree of perfection which belongs to it, but not *formally* or *actually.* In this case, the being in which it is found is not in potentiality in respect of it, but on the contrary in act after a higher fashion. Its superiority is, so to speak, an obstacle which prevents the thing which it virtually contains from being present with its proper and inferior determination (*formality*).

Thus the perfections of all corporeal objects exist

modern philosophers themselves, and still more between the modern philosophers and the ancients, with their formal terminology.

It may also be observed that certain philosophic terms understood in a material sense, have acquired a meaning totally different from their original significance. Take, for example, the term *object.* For the ancients the *object* meant *what is placed before the mind* or presented to it, considered formally as such. Hence imaginary beings, the *chimaera* for example, were said to exist *objectively* or as objects present to the mind, but not *really* or as things existing outside the mind. The moderns, on the contrary, understand by an *object* the thing itself or the *subject* which is presented to the mind, and to exist objectively is therefore the same as to exist really or outside the mind.

[1] Observe, however, that the expression *potentially, in potentia,* is sometimes used improperly in the sense of *virtually.*

virtually in God, conclusions are virtually contained in the premisses, partial lives exist virtually in the life of an organism.

(c) We must now call attention to the fact that the contrast between *implicit* and *explicit* is not to be confused with that between *virtual* and *formal* (*actual*). A thing contained implicitly in another may be there formally or actually, not virtually : but it is present in a confused fashion, wrapped up and hidden as a flower lies hidden and folded in the bud. For example, in the truth *Peter is a man* there is implicitly contained the further truth *Peter is a rational animal*.

(d) Finally a thing given formally and explicitly may be in act in two different ways. Take, for instance, a man who is running as fast as he can to escape his enemies. If I say *he is fleeing* I mention what he is doing *in express act* (*in actu signato*) (what he is doing as stressed or expressed, so to speak, by his intention). If, however, I say that *he is accelerating the rate of his breathing* I mention what he is doing only *in accomplished act* (*in actu exercito*).

Similarly, a man who reads Ronsard, Lamartine, or Victor Hugo, to count the number of times they use the words *aimer* or *chérir*, reads the poets, to be sure, and reads them formally and explicitly, but that is not what he does in intention. On the contrary, when we consider his object in reading the poets, we must say that he is preparing an essay of *stylometric* literary criticism. We may say that he reads the poets in effect or in accomplished act, but that expressly or in express act he is preparing the essay in question.

Again, when we repeat *lilia agri non laborant neque nent*, thinking solely of the meaning of the sentence, what we then know in express act is *the lilies of the field,* which are present to our mind as *neither toiling nor spinning.* But at the same time we know in accomplished act *the nominative plural, lilia,* which in turn we shall know in express act, if we return to the sentence in question and submit it to grammatical analysis.

That is to say, the phrase *in express act* (*in actu signato*) is used of things to which intellect or will are directed, when they are the object of a concept of the intellect or an intention of the will specially formed for them, and are thus presented to the mind or brought into being under the actual heading or on the actual ground expressed by their name. When on the contrary they are presented to the mind or brought into being on occasion of something else and without being intended in themselves, we say that they are present only *in accomplished act* (*in actu exercito*).

VIII

THEODICY (NATURAL THEOLOGY)

METAPHYSICS studies being as such, but for that very reason is obliged to study the cause of being. That is why its highest branch, the coping-stone so to speak of the entire metaphysical edifice, is concerned with him who is subsistent Being itself. This branch of metaphysics is called *natural theology* (the science of God in so far as he is accessible to natural reason, or, from another point of view, so far as he is the cause of things and author of the natural order). Since Leibniz it has also been known by the less appropriate name *theodicy*.

Leibniz in his *Theodicy* (1710) undertook to defend Divine Providence against the attacks of the sceptics (particularly Bayle). The term *theodicy* (etymologically : *justification of God*) has been used since that time to denote the branch of philosophy whose object is God. But the name is objectionable on two grounds : first because the providence of God has no need to be *justified* by philosophers ; secondly because providence and the problem of evil are neither the sole nor the most important questions of which natural theology has to treat.

The primary questions discussed by natural theology are obviously those which concern God's existence itself.

For the existence of God is not in fact, as Malebranche and the ontologists believed, evident to us immediately and prior to any discursive activity of the mind ; it is in virtue of that intellectual operation which is the activity most profoundly distinctive of man, namely *ratiocination*, that it becomes evident to us, and to attain that certainty reasoning must proceed not from the mere idea or notion of perfect being (the ontological argument of St. Anselm and Descartes) but from facts whose existence is established beyond dispute. St. Thomas, resuming the entire tradition of the past, shows by five different arguments how the conclusion *God exists* is imposed with absolute necessity on the human reason. There exist in the world motion or change ; beings and events newly brought into being ; things which are and are capable of not being ; things graded in degrees of perfection, whose perfection, which consists in being, is more or less limited, obscured, mingled with imperfection ; irrational natures disposed towards an object or end, as is proved, not only by the complex system of the universe or the structure of living organisms, but even by the simple aptitude of every agent to produce its specific operation. To account for these various facts we are compelled—for under pain of absurdity we are obliged to stop at an ultimate explanation of existence —to admit a cause which moves without being moved, causes without being caused, cannot lack existence, contains in its purity the perfection of which things partake in greater or less degree, possesses an intellect which is the final ground of all natures and the first principle of all things. Such a cause we term *God* ; it is pure act, deriving its existence from itself (*a se*). In other words, *being* itself is its nature or essence, it is *subsistent Being itself, he who is*. This conclusion, which for the philosopher involves the most sublime truths of metaphysics, is reached very simply by common sense, for it is in truth the most fundamental natural operation of the human understanding, so that it can be denied only by denying reason itself and its first principles (the laws of *identity* or non-contradiction, *sufficient reason, causality*) ; and as the history of philosophy shows only too plainly, the mind has no other choice than between the alternatives : " the true God or radical irrationality." [1]

It is also the province of theodicy to show with what manner of knowledge we know God and in due course to study his nature and perfections, in particular the *unity, simplicity,* and *immutability* which are immediately deducible from the perfection of underived existence (*aseity*), the fundamental character of pure act, and which prove most clearly that he is absolutely and essentially distinct from the world ; his relations with the world, his knowledge, his activity as Creator and Mover ; and finally the problems involved in the divine foreknowledge of contingent events, particularly man's free acts, and those arising out of the existence of evil in the universe.

The school of *Aristotle and St. Thomas* teaches that God is known by the natural reason analogically, so that we perceive the divine perfections (*being, unity, goodness, wisdom, love,* etc.) in the mirror of creatures, without asserting any unity of nature, common measure, or proportion, or mixture or confusion of any kind between God and created things. This

---

[1] Garrigou-Lagrange, *Dieu, son existence, sa nature,* Paris, 3rd ed., 1920.

teaching is opposed to two contrary errors, the error of the *agnostics*, who maintain that the Divine Being is beyond the ken of our intellect and God unknowable by the reason (sceptics ; phenomenalists ; positivists like Comte and Spencer, the Kantian school as a whole), and the error of the *pantheists*, who confuse the Divine Being with the being of created things (Parmenides, Heraclitus, the Stoics, Spinoza, the German metaphysicians after Lessing and Kant ; the modernists and *immanentists*).

Philosophy of Aristotle and St. Thomas

God is known by analogy and is absolutely distinct from creatures.

Pantheism	*Agnosticism*
God confused with creatures.	God unknowable.

IX

THE aim of the *practical* sciences is to know, not for the sake of knowing, but to procure by some action the good of man (other than the pure act of knowing truth). But the *good of man* can be understood in two different senses ; either of *this or that particular good* or of the good which is in itself alone *the good* of man and which, as we say, determines the significance of human life.

THE PHILOSOPHY OF ART

Of the different practical sciences which are concerned with the good of man from the first standpoint (that of particular goods, and not of the absolute good of human life), none, as we have pointed out already,[1] is a philosophy. For none of these proposes to regulate human action in reference to the supreme cause in the practical order, that is (for in the practical order the aim or end pursued fulfils the function of cause or principle) in reference to the last end (the absolute good of man).

Nor are these practical sciences *sciences* in the strict sense, for they do not proceed by way of demonstration, drawing conclusions from their premises.

[1] See p. 149.

They are rather arts than sciences, and belong immediately to the wide category of art, not to that of science.

The essential character of art taken in its complete extension is to instruct us how to make something, so that it is constructed, formed, or arranged, as it ought to be, and thus to secure the perfection or goodness, not of the maker, but of the object itself which he makes. Art therefore belongs to the practical order in the sense that it instructs us how to make something, considering not the use we should make of our free will but the manner in which the work as such and in itself should be executed. We may thus say that art is concerned with what is to be made, *factibile*, ποιητόν.

This formal character of *making* is fulfilled primarily in the material objects produced or fashioned by man (the *factibile* in the strict sense). But in a wider sense it is to be found also in works of a purely spiritual nature. In this case it goes beyond the sphere of practice as such, so far as practice is opposed to speculation and signifies an activity other than that of pure knowing. It is in this sense that there is making in the purely speculative order (a form of argument, a proposition, are works, but works of the speculative reason), and there are arts, logic, for example, which are speculative arts.

In order, however, to establish a general theory of art and *making* we must have recourse to the highest and most universal concepts and principles of human knowledge. Such a theory therefore belongs to the domain of philosophy.

The province of philosophy thus defined is indeed

practical, since it is concerned with making, and its object is to order from above the branches of practical instruction. Nevertheless, since it is in the strict sense a science, it cannot be essentially practical, but remains essentially speculative in virtue of its object and method of procedure ; moreover, it is extremely remote from actual practice. Indeed, not only has it no concern with the application of the rules of art to a particular work to be accomplished, but further it formulates rules which are far too general to be capable of such immediate application and to be correctly termed rules of art in the strict sense ; it is therefore practical only in an improper sense and very imperfectly.

The individual arts alone (branches of study essentially practical) possess rules sufficiently detailed to be immediately applicable to a particular work, and their application belongs solely to them. Further, with the exception of the fine arts, whose object, beauty, being itself universal and immaterial, enables philosophy to perform effectively though from a remote height her office of supreme arbiter, the arts since they are devoid of any universal character, except the fact of being arts, of which philosophers can take cognizance, escape her jurisdiction almost completely.

If we would accurately describe this branch of philosophy, we should term it the *philosophy of making*, but we shall call it simply the *philosophy of art*.[1] Here

---

[1] The term *aesthetics*, which has now become current, would be doubly incorrect here. Modern writers understand by the word *the theory of beauty and art*, as though the philosophy of art were the place in which to treat questions concerning beauty considered in itself (such questions belong to ontology), and as though art were confined to the fine arts (a mistake which vitiates the entire theory of art). Moreover,

we must first inquire what is the nature of art, if it is indeed, as St. Thomas teaches, *a virtue of the practical intellect*, and how it is distinguished on the one hand from the *speculative* virtues (*understanding of first principles, knowledge, wisdom*), on the other from the *moral* virtues, *prudence* in particular ; how art is to be subdivided and the different art classifie d ; and finally what are the first principles and distinctive conditions—though solely of the highest and most general order—of those arts which have beauty for their object (the *fine arts*) and which thus occupy a superior rank among the arts.

ETHICS

The practical science which aims at procuring man's unqualified good, his absolute good, is that of *morals* or *ethics*. Since its distinctive object is not the

the word *aesthetics* is derived etymologically from sensibility (αἰσθάνομαι = *feel*), whereas art, and beauty also, are matters of the intellect, quite as much as of feeling.

Scholastic textbooks do not usually devote a separate treatise to the philosophy of art, and either study its problems in psychology alone, or, the better to explain the concept of prudence, in ethics. It would be necessary to classify the philosophy of art, like ethics itself, under natural philosophy, if we kept to the single standpoint of the specification of the sciences by their formal object. But if we adopt the wider standpoint of the end to which the sciences are ordered, we must distinguish practical from speculative philosophy, and it is equally necessary to distinguish, in practical philosophy, the philosophy of making and the philosophy of doing (*cf.* the author's *Art and Scholasticism*). This treatment presents the double advantage of corresponding to a very marked trend of modern thought, which tends to devote a special treatise (aesthetics) to the theory of art, and of returning to one of Aristotle's fundamental classifications : πᾶσα διάνοια ἢ πρακτικὴ ἢ ποιητικὴ ἢ θεωρητική (*Metaph.*, ii, 1, 1025 b 25). *Cf. Top.*, vi, 6, 145 a 15, and viii, 1, 157 a 10 ; *Metaph.*, vi, 1 ; *Nic. Eth.*, vi, 2, 1139 a 27. Hamelin (*op. cit.*, pp. 81 *sqq.*) makes a convincing defence against Zeller of Aristotle's real opinion on this matter.

perfection of the works produced and fashioned by man but the good and perfection of the agent himself, or the use he freely makes of his faculties, it is in the strict sense the science of *action*, the science of human acts (in technical language, of the *agibile* or πρακτόν, that is to say, of the free use, so far as it is free, of our faculties).

Ethics is as practical as any true science in the strict sense can be, for it teaches not only the most general rules of remote application, but also the particular rules applicable to the particular action to be performed.

But at the same time this science has in view, not some particular secondary end, but the last end (the absolute good) of man, the supreme cause in the practical order. It is therefore a philosophy. It is without qualification the practical philosophy.

Note.—Though ethics is as practical as any science in the strict sense can be, we must not therefore suppose that it is essentially practical (no science *vere et proprie dicta* is essentially practical), or that it is sufficient to make men behave rightly. It supplies, it is true, rules immediately applicable to particular cases, but it has no power to make us constantly apply them as we should in particular cases,[1] in spite of the difficulties

---

[1] On the contrary, the essentially practical sciences, that is to say the arts, themselves apply their rules to particular cases. These sciences are, strictly speaking, practical, but are not sciences in the strict sense but only improperly.

There are thus many degrees of practicality. The philosophy of art (whose end is practical, and whose object an *operabile*, but to be known) provides no rules immediately applicable to particular cases. It is only improperly and very imperfectly practical.

Ethics (whose end is practical, and whose object is also an *operabile*, but also to be known) does not apply, but provides rules immediately applicable to particular cases. It is as practical as a science in the

arising from our passions and the complexity of material circumstances. It remains, therefore, essentially speculative in its final object (*knowledge* of human acts) and in its procedure (the deduction of truths from their premisses, not incitement to action) and is thus practical only in an improper sense.[1] If man is to do the right in the order of action moral science must be supplemented by the virtue of *prudence*, which, if we make use of it, makes us always *judge* correctly of the act we should perform, and *will* always that which we have thus judged to be right.

On the other hand, ethics only supplies rules of human conduct in the natural order and in relation to man's last end as it would be, if it were a natural happiness. But since, in fact, man's last end is a supernatural good (*God possessed* not by the imperfect knowledge of human reason as such, but by *the*

strict sense can be practical, but it is not strictly speaking or perfectly practical.

The arts—*medicine*, for example, or *engineering*—whose object is something to be done (not merely an *operabile*, but envisaged *operabiliter*), provide rules immediately applicable and actually apply them to particular cases, but only by enabling us to judge of what is to be done, not by making us will to do it (for the artist can make a mistake and still be an artist (because he wills to make it). They are in the strict sense practical—but do not attain the highest degree of practicability.

Finally *prudence* (whose object is also something to be done) applies to particular cases the rules of moral science and reason, not only teaching us to judge of the act to be performed, but making us employ as we ought our free activity (for *the prudent man*, as such, always wills the right). It is, strictly speaking, practical, and attains the highest degree of practicability.

[1] *Cf.* St. Thomas, *Sup. Boet. de Trin.*, q. 5, a. 1, *ad* 3 : *Scientia moralis, quamvis sit propter operationem, tamen illa operatio non est actus scientiae, sed actus virtutis, ut patet V Ethic. Unde non potest dici ars, sed magis in illis operationibus se habet virtus loco artis et ideo veteres diffinierunt virtutem esse artem bene recteque vivendi, ut dicit August. X, de Civ. Dei.*

beatific and deifying vision of the Divine Essence), and since his actions must be regulated in reference to this supernatural end and so as to enable him to attain it, ethics or philosophic morality is evidently inadequate to teach him everything he needs to know in order to act rightly. It must be completed and elevated by the teachings of revelation.

The epithet *practical*, applied to ethics, does not merely mean *having as its aim an activity other than that of simply knowing* (in this sense *practical*, whether used of art or morals, is opposed to *speculative*) ; but more strictly concerned with *action and behaviour* (the πρακτόν, the distinctive sphere of moral science and the moral virtues as contrasted with the ποιητόν, the distinctive sphere of art).

The fundamental question which practical philosophy must answer before any other is in what consists (from the standpoint of the natural order) the last end or absolute good of man. It must then study the actions by which man approaches or departs from his last end, examining first their nature and inner machinery, then what constitutes their moral character, that is to say, renders them morally good or bad. Ethics must, therefore, study in themselves the supreme rule of such actions (questions which treat of the eternal law and the natural law) and *their immediate rule* (questions relating to the conscience); it must also study *the intrinsic principles* from which those acts proceed, that is to say, the moral virtues and vices.

But since ethics is a practical science it must not be content with these universal considerations ; it must proceed to the more particular determination of human acts and their rules. It is therefore obliged to study in great detail the rules which regulate man's conduct first so far as they concern *the good of the agent himself* and secondly so far as they concern *the good of others* (consequently the virtue of *justice*).

The latter inquiry introduces a number of most important questions pertaining to what is called *natural right*, and treating in the first place of man's obligations to God (a question of natural religion),[1] secondly of his obligations to his fellow-men. Here are discussed the questions which concern men as individuals (*the rights of the individual*, for example, *the right of property*), and those which concern them as members of a natural whole whose common good individuals must serve—the family and the political society (the *rights of society*).

Aristotle divided the science of morality, of human conduct (*ethics* in the wide sense) into three parts : the science of man's actions as an individual, *ethics* (in the stricter sense) ; the science of his actions as a member of the domestic society, *economics* ; the science of his actions as a member of the city (the civil society), *politics*.[2]

On the fundamental question of ethics—the question of man's last end—we find for the last time the schools of philosophy divided roughly into three groups.

The school of *Aristotle and St. Thomas* teaches that the entire moral life depends on man's tendency to his sovereign good or happiness and that the object

[1] I.e. of religion as it would be apart from the supernatural order to which man has in fact been raised.

[2] See on this point *Nic. Eth.*, vi, 9, 1142 a 9 ; *Eud. Eth.*, i, 8, 1218 b 13, and the two first chapters of the *Politics*. *Cf*. Hamelin, *op. cit.*, p. 85.

in which this happiness consists is God—whom, more-over, we ought to love, not for our own sake, but for himself (precisely because he is our last end, that is to say, that which is willed and loved for itself, not for the sake of anything beyond).

The schools which find the end and rule of human conduct in *pleasure* (*hedonism*, Aristippus, Epicurus), *utility* (*utilitarianism*, Bentham, John Stuart Mill), the *state* (Hegel and *sociologists*), *humanity* (Auguste Comte), *progress* (Herbert Spencer), *sympathy* (the Scottish school), *pity* (Schopenhauer) or the production of the *superman* (Nietzsche), assign as man's last end some-thing created, and thereby degrade him below himself.

The schools which claim that *virtue* (the Stoics, Spinoza) or *duty* (Kant) is self-sufficient, either because *virtue* is itself *happiness,* or because the pursuit of *happiness* is immoral, assign as man's last end *man* himself, and thereby, while seeming to deify man, really, like the schools last mentioned, degrade him below himself, for the greatness of man consists in the fact that his sole end is the uncreated Good.

Thomist Philosophy
(*Ethics of Happiness or the Sovereign Good*)
Man is ordered to a last end other than himself, and this last end is God.

Moral Systems which degrade Man	*Moral Systems which deify Man*
Man is ordered to a last end other than himself, and this end is something created (*hedonism, Epicureanism, utilitarianism,* etc.).	Man is not ordered to any last end other than himself, his own *virtue* being his last end (*Stoicism*), or his goodness not depending on any good for which he has been made (*Kantism*).

Thus on every one of the great problems of philosophy the doctrine of Aristotle and St. Thomas, when compared with the doctrines of other philosophers, appears as an eminence between two contrary errors. This is an additional argument for its truth to be added to those enumerated earlier.[1]

The truth, indeed, is not to be found in a philosophy which keeps the mean between contrary errors by its mediocrity and by falling below them, being built up by borrowing from both, balancing one against another and mingling them by arbitrary choices made without the light of a guiding principle (*eclecticism*); it must be sought in a philosophy which keeps the mean between contrary errors by its superiority, dominating both, so that they appear as fragments fallen and severed from its unity. For it is clear that, if this philosophy be true, it must reveal in full what error sees only in part and distorted by a bias, and thus must judge and secure, by its own principles, and in the light of its own truth, whatever truth error contains though it cannot distinguish.

[1] See pp. 99–101.

CONCLUSION

PHILOSOPHY is thus divided into three principal sections : *logic, speculative philosophy, practical philosophy* ; or, if we take account of the subdivisions of these three sections, into seven main sections : *minor logic, major logic ;* the *philosophy of mathematics,* the *philosophy of nature, metaphysics ;* the *philosophy of art* and *ethics.* This order is represented by the following table :

I LOGIC	1. *Minor* or *formal logic :* the rules of reasoning
	2. *Major* or *material logic :* the matter of reasoning

II SPECULATIVE PHILOSOPHY	3. The *philosophy of mathematics :* quantity
	4. The *philosophy of nature :* { the material world } *cosmology* { man *psychology*
	5. *Metaphysics* { truth (epistemology) *criticism* / being in general *ontology* / being *a se* (natural theology) *theodicy*

III PRACTICAL PHILOSOPHY	6. The *philosophy of art :* making
	7. *Ethics* or *moral philosophy :* action, conduct

The division of philosophy into *speculative* and *practical* depends, not on the specific character of the various philosophic sciences, but on the end which they pursue. If that end is knowledge alone, the philosophy is speculative ; if the good of man, it is practical.[1]

If the philosophic sciences are classified from the standpoint of their specific character,[2] *ethics,* which

---

[1] See St. Thomas, *Sup. Boet. de Trin.,* q. 5, *ad* 4.
[2] This specification depends essentially on the degree of abstraction or degree of immateriality of the object studied.

treats of the moral virtues [1] and whose formal object is human *action*, and the *philosophy of art*, which treats of the practical intellectual virtues and whose formal object is human *making*, are divisions of the science of man, which itself belongs to *natural philosophy* (though it enters also into *metaphysics*).   From this point of view we can recognise as specifically distinct philosophic sciences only *logic*, *metaphysics*, and the *philosophy of nature*, also the *philosophy of mathematics*, if this is not regarded as a subdivision of *metaphysics* or of the *philosophy of nature*.

[1] *Sic pertinet ad philosophiam (naturalem), et est pars illius, quia agit de anima ut est actus corporis, et consequenter de moralibus ejus.* (John of St. Thomas, *Cursus. phil.*, i, p. 732 ; *Log.*, ii, q. 27, a. 1.)